Suck Less at Love:

She Said, He Said Advice on Relationships

Cyndi Lewis

Copyright © 2024 by Cyndi Lewis

All rights reserved. Published in the United States of America by REL Print Group, *A Hezzie Mae Publication*, Duluth, MN. www.HezzieMae.com

No part of this book may be use or reproduced in any manner without written permission from the publisher.

Cover Photography: Bailey Jo Tardy, www.baileyjophotographymn.com

Cyndi Lewis

Suck Less at Love

For Andrew, my husband and the love of my life. I put dibs on dying first because I don't want to live in this world without you . . . but, if you happen to die first, I'm marrying for money.

TABLE OF CONTENTS

Introduction 1

Chapter 1: The Meet-Cute 5

Chapter 2: The Backstory Timeline 15

Chapter 3: What is Love? 27

Chapter 4: Attraction and Relationships 37

Chapter 5: What Kind of Intimacy Currency Is in Your Wallet? 51

Chapter 6: Trying to Change Him Will Make You Miserable 59

Chapter 7: Men Are Inherently Lazy 75

Chapter 8: Set Expectations Up Front 85

Chapter 9: Actions Will Show You His True Feelings 99

Chapter 10: If You Keep Score, You'll Never Win 111

Chapter 11: Perfection in Imperfection 121

Chapter 12: Communicate, Communicate, and Communicate Some More 135

Chapter 13: Your Partner Should NOT Be Your Best Friend 151

Chapter 14: "He Won't Bring You Flowers Anymore," the Nasty Naysayers Say 165

Chapter 15: One Key to Rule Them All 177

Chapter 16: The Fairytale Future 187

Epilogue 193

Bibliography 209

Introduction

Love advice is very take-it-or-leave-it, regardless of where it's coming from. For the right message to reach the person who needs it most, that person needs to be open to new perspectives and constructive criticisms. A PhD or a job as a marriage counselor is not required to give great advice about love and relationships. The people who should be the most qualified to give advice about love and relationships are the people with successful lived experiences in the subject matter.

My husband Andrew and I are that kind of couple, the one people observe and wonder what it is that makes us so blissfully successful in our relationship and the one that makes people say, "I want what they have." Both having had unsuccessful first marriages, we came together later in life with enough emotional maturity, confidence, and experience to set us up for success. If our relationship were a meme, it would be a photo of us with the caption #couplegoals. Take it from my best friend, who is still on her quest to find the love of her life. While she gets frustrated with her dating and relationship experiences, she tells me, "Your relationship is the only one I've ever seen in real life that makes me believe that love and successful relationships are possible."

Why should you take my advice? I'm just a girl who has experienced over forty years of life, had two children, been married, divorced, and remarried, and is trying to live life without regrets. I finally found the happiness that I had always hoped and believed existed, and I have been giving the same advice over and over again to friends who seem to be facing the same issues that I and many other women have had.

While I care deeply about my friends to whom I am giving this relationship advice, I am not the "yes woman" type of sugar-coating friend. I'm the friend who warns you up front that the advice that I give might not be what you want to hear, and it may sting a little, but I'm telling you the truth out of genuine love and concern for your overall happiness. Recently, I told my best friend that if she makes the same dating mistake again, I will find a jack-in-the-box that has a hand that pops out and bitch slaps the user in the face, and I'll send it to her since I can't do it in person. No, I wouldn't actually slap her, but I wanted to illustrate to her how passionately I feel about snapping her out of her cycle of mistakes.

I'm one of the biggest cheerleaders for love and happiness in relationships, and I want to be able to help as many people experience what I've found. The caveat to that help and advice is that some things that I say may not be popular or easy to hear, but someone needs to speak up and give it to you straight, and that person is me. Luckily for you, however, it's not just my perspective that you'll be pondering in this book. You'll also be getting a man's perspective from my hubby.

Andrew, my second husband, described me in his wedding vows as being "filled with fairytale dreams" and that I have a "light that lights up the world." He said, "When I was looking for someone to be with, there were a lot of dark times looking for you. I was holding off and not taking anyone because I was looking for that light that you brought to me, and I want to thank you for doing that because I don't think I would have gotten there on my own." Surely, the woman lucky enough to be described like that must know something about love.

When I asked my hubby to do this project with me, his response was, "Why do you want my perspective? I'm not an expert." No, he's not an expert, but neither am I. Andy is a rare commodity because he falls into the 10 percent of men who have alpha male status. For years, he was the bad boy, a wild stallion that so many women tried to tame but failed. He has kissed a lot of girls, and most of his relationships were initiated by women, not by him. Advice on relationships from this kind of man is pretty valuable, especially since he's not going to tell me what I want to hear.

Having no agenda other than to participate in this project because he loves me, and I asked him to, Andy is honest and blunt. In so many instances, I have wasted my breath giving a friend the same advice over and over again, only to have them ask, "What does

Andy think about it?" He can give them the same advice that I did, but since it came from him, they start to listen. Go figure.

In this book, you are getting a two-for-one deal or BOGO, and we all love a good deal. Our collective opinions on success in relationships will be presented in a she said, he said format. Every chapter starts out with my perspective on the topic and is followed by an unfiltered interview with my hubby about the subject matter. After the end-of-chapter summaries, there will be a smattering of questions reluctantly provided by my husband. The questions are intended to get you thinking introspectively about the subject to aid in the sucking less as needed in that area of relationships.

As a way of helping visualize the scenarios or role-playing references, I will be using the fictitious couple, Dick and Jane. Dick and Jane have been married for twenty years. She feels like he doesn't listen or help her, and he is frustrated because he feels like he's always getting yelled at and he doesn't get as much intimacy as he wants. They are both frustrated, but they have children and want to find a way to love each other more and suck less in their relationship.

We hope (well, I do, since he wasn't a willing participant) that our advice will help you, Dick, and Jane to find more joy and love in your relationships.

Chapter 1: The Meet-Cute

SHE SAID

What is a meet-cute? It's a cute story of how two people meet. Who in her right mind would have a meet-cute that started with her soon-to-be ex-husband in the room? Me. Oh yeah, it's not your typical love story, but it is one of my very favorite stories to tell.

Let me preface this story by saying that my ex-husband and I had filed our divorce paperwork at the courthouse together, but the divorce had not yet been finalized, and I had not moved out into my own place yet.

One afternoon, as my soon-to-be ex and I were sitting on opposite ends of the same room in the house we bought together, I noticed him scrolling on his iPad through profiles on dating apps. Because it was shaping up to be an amicable divorce, I asked, "Are you finding anyone normal?" He and I had met on Match.com in the early 2000s, so it was only natural that we would revert to a method of dating that we knew—online dating.

"Yeah," he responded.

"Do you mind sharing with me the app that has the most normal people on it?" I questioned.

"Zoosk," he replied curtly.

"Do you mind if I use that one too?"

"No." Within a short while, I heard him say, "Hey, your profile just popped up on my iPad."

"Don't read it!" I begged.

"Oh, I'm reading it," he said defiantly. "You sound bitchy."

Well, of course, I'm going to sound that way to the person I just asked for a divorce.

As I started scrolling and swiping, my excitement quickly faded. My visions of this perfect new mate dissipated with every poorly lit selfie, every flannel shirt, every balding head, and every droopy dad bod. In the years of my marriage, when I became unhappy, I started a mental log of traits that my perfect man would have if I ever found myself single again. It was quickly becoming evident that I would never find what I'd dreamed existed. When I told my friends about my divorce, their response was a collective, "I wouldn't want to be dating again, especially at our age." No way could it be as bad as they forewarned. Clearly, I was in denial as I started to shop, my smile quickly changing to a meh face. It WAS as bad as they had predicted. Maybe I had made the wrong decision.

Wait . . . wait a minute. Who is this?

"Andrew, 147 miles away," read the text superimposed over the photo of a stoically handsome police officer leaning up against a police department horse trailer. Helloooooo . . . Andrew. He lives 147 miles away . . . dang it! Oh well, you only live once.

I felt my temperature rise, my heart race, and my face flush with excitement as I sent him a message.

"Hello! Your profile made me laugh, but I see you're 147 miles away, so if distance is going to be an issue, just don't write back. I just moved, I'm moving again soon, and I have little kids, so I'm not moving again."

I know . . . I'm blunt, but I pride myself on my efficiency.

"Well, let's just see where this goes," he responded.

And that was that. September 2, 2018, he was mine—he just didn't know it yet. We exchanged rapid-fire messages on the app until I got annoyed at the typing and the waiting. I hate waiting, and I am too old to be able to type super-fast on a smartphone, so I asked him if he would give me a call instead.

"People don't do that this early," was his honest response.

"Well, I'm not like most people, and calling is more efficient," I explained.

"I'm brushing my teeth," he texted. "Now I'm flossing."

Seriously? Was he a real person? Come on, guy.

That first phone call turned into a constant stream of text messages during the day and four-hour-long conversations on the phone in the evenings. We couldn't learn enough about each other fast enough. It was like feeling starved, and the other person was food, but no matter how much you ate, you never got full.

Meeting up wasn't the easiest task because Andrew lived over two hours away, and I had to schedule around my children's custody schedule and our misaligning work schedules. Truth be told, in my short few seconds of singledom, I had written more than one name on my dance card. I was single after sixteen years, and I wanted options.

Roughly two weeks from the day we matched on the app, I asked if Andy wanted to come for a day date up to the city I was living in on Labor Day—the weekend I was moving into my new, single-life house. The Saturday and Sunday before Labor Day, I had dates lined up with other potential suitors, but as the weekend drew nearer, the others didn't seem to be in contention anymore. Ignoring my very conservative Baptist upbringing, I lost the battle to my newly single self's emotions, and I asked him if he wanted to come up for the whole weekend . . . to stay at my house . . . a stranger. *Gasp! Clutch your pearls, ladies.*

I know, it sounds so bad. I swear that was not normal behavior for me. Of course, my mom thought I'd lost my damn mind and demanded a phone call every fifteen minutes so she could pacify herself with the reassurance that I wasn't being murdered. I can vividly recall sitting in my sunroom with a stomach full of excited butterflies that induced a whole-body tremble. Was he who he said he was? Is he too good to be true? *What if he IS a serial killer? What was I thinking?! I'm insane.*

A white Cadillac sedan turned into my driveway, and I stopped breathing. It was happening! Somehow, I ended up at the back door, not knowing what or who would walk through, and suddenly, there he was: the man in the photos. Confidently and silently, he strode into my house without a word, grabbed me in a tight embrace, and breathed me in. It was electric. Honestly, it was a blur after that, but I will admit that what happened made us late for our dinner reservations.

In the haze of that weekend, it seemed like we were the only two people left on the face of the earth. Nothing else existed outside of the nest we were in. The next morning, Andy received a text from his partner at work, "Did she steal your kidneys yet?" *Funny. Who even had time to check if we had our kidneys? What were kidneys again?*

In the last few hours together, I found myself grasping for a way to prolong the warm fuzzies.

"So, what do I call you now?" I asked, hoping for the answer I wanted to hear.

"You can call me anything you want," he answered.

"Okay, you're my boyfriend now," I informed him in a chipper tweet. And so, it started . . . the beginning of the greatest love story of my life.

HE SAID

She: What is a meet-cute?

He: What is a what?

She: A meet-cute.

He: I don't know what a meet-cute is. I've never heard those two words put together.

She: (*Laughing uncontrollably*) It's the cute story of how people meet.

He: Oh. I think that needs to be phrased differently.

She: (*Still laughing so hard I can't breathe*) Okay . . .

He: That's the dumbest thing . . . nobody's ever going to pick up on that. (*Sarcastically*) A meet-cute. What is a meet-cute? Usually, people refer to it as "our story" or "How did you guys meet?" It's not called a meet-cute.

She: Okay, this clearly is going nowhere. What is your recollection of how we met?

He: It was online. That's how it all started.

She: There's more to it than that.

He: No, there isn't. I don't understand.

She: How do you remember it going down?

He: I don't remember it going down. We met online. You just started messaging me, and then you just called me right away.

She: You called me.

He: Well, I don't know what happened. I thought you called me, but . . .

She: Well, you were texting me for like two weeks beforehand.

He: (*Surprised*) Oh, really? Are you sure?

She: I'm one hundred percent positive.

He: I'm pretty sure you like texted twice and then called me.

She: Oh yeah, the night of, but I'm talking about the span between reaching out on the app until the end of the first weekend together. That's . . .

He: I have no idea what the hell you're talking about. How can it be more involved than just meeting online and frickin' talking to each other? (*Chuckling*) And then meeting. There can't be any more than that.

Both: (*Laughing together at the clear lack of miscommunication.*)

She: I just can't with you right now. Okay, do you remember that first weekend you met me at my house?

He: Well, yeah.

She: What was your takeaway about a possible relationship at the end of that weekend?

He: I didn't really think about it like that, I don't think.

She: How did you think about it then because I pretty much nailed you down as being my boyfriend at the end of that?

He: I was just like, that was fun. I didn't know if it would happen again. I don't remember.

She: Even though you were technically my boyfriend . . . officially?

He: Yeah, in your mind, I'm sure I was.

She: I asked you, and you said that was fine!

He: I've told you this before: I would have told you whatever you wanted to hear to get where I needed to get, and at that point, I had to keep the doors open. I wasn't like, "OOH, this is the one!" I didn't think that way.

She: Well, that's too bad because that's what I thought.

He: That's why you should write the book because you're not gonna hear what you want to hear from me.

If you could listen to this recorded interview, you'd be dying with laughter. This first dialogue illustrates perfectly how differently men's and women's brains can work. Time passes differently for some than it does for others. Often, women see the details and get lost in them. On the other hand, some men remember the high-level concepts; thus, time goes faster for them because they don't get stuck ruminating about every moment.

I had idealized our meeting into this epic love story, and all he remembers is meeting online and talking. Were we even in the same house that first weekend? He's brutally honest, I told you, and that's why his perspective on relationships is important and relevant to my advice about love.

Perspective can affect so much of how we remember and perceive the world. Hopefully, our opposing but collective perspectives will help you navigate your relationship and find ways to make it as fulfilling and wonderful as ours has become.

Chapter 2: The Backstory Timeline

SHE SAID & HE SAID

To understand the book in the context of my evolving relationship, you need to have a little understanding of our relationship timeline. Additionally, the chapters are not laid out chronologically to the stages in our relationship, and without this information, you would likely be lost, and that would mean that I sucked at writing this book in a way that made any sense.

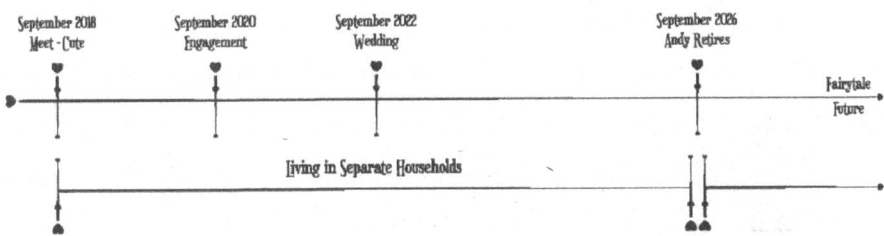

From the moment that Andy and I met until the day we got engaged, I agonized over whether or not I was emotionally strong enough to be in a long-distance relationship. I had gone from college, where I was being taken care of by my dad, right to being taken care of by my first husband, to being shot out on the other end alone with two children after my divorce. Having a relationship where I wouldn't be able to rely on my significant other for everything that I was used to someone else taking care of was only part of the reason I was not handling long-distance well.

When I decide I want something, I want it all, and I want it yesterday. The start of my relationship with Andy was so emotionally difficult because I couldn't be near him when most people try to be with each other the most. Should I try to make it work? Is it going to be worth it?

"Why can't you find someone that lives closer to you?" my parents asked.

"Um, have you looked at who's available at my age in a small town? No," I rationalized.

While I was certain of what my decision should be in my response to my parents, I was less sure that I could make it work. I knew he was my person, but the separation was killing me . . . it made my chest feel tight when we weren't together—it WAS physically killing me.

After a dinner out with one of my dear friends, we were sitting in my car trying to talk through whether or not Andy was worth the pain and emotional distress of dealing with a long-distance relationship.

"But when he holds me, he kind of squeezes me, and it just feels . . . right," I explained to her.

In the nanosecond pause in the conversation, the lyrics "You've gotta hold her, you've gotta squeeze her, you have to try, you've got to try . . ." played through the car's speakers, and our eyes shot open, our jaws dropped, and we were struck speechless as we stared at each other.

"Oh. My. Gosh! It's a sign. He's the one. You need to make this work!" she excitedly exclaimed as we both hopped up and down like children who had consumed too much sugar.

I'm not an I-believe-in-signs kind of person, but Michael Bublé was clearly trying to tell me through his song "Try a Little Tenderness" that I needed to do everything I could to endure the long distance because Andy was worth it. For someone with an intense borderline-obsessive personality like mine, sticking it out was definitely going to be one of the hardest struggles and triumphs of my life.

The great thing, however, about long-distance relationships is the forced communication because that's all you have. Real feelings and connections cannot be clouded by physical distance because you spend most of the time miles apart. How did Andy feel about the long-distance aspect of our relationship?

"I just remember saying that we would work it out and that it would be okay because the time apart would go quickly. I've explained to you. For me, time moves very quickly because I live in the moment. I think that after we got married, you stopped being as worried about the long distance because you had the security of commitment. You still complained that something always seemed to break when I wasn't there, but that allowed you to become more independent and find other resources to help you solve those problems," explained Andy as we rehashed the past.

In other words, he was fine with it. Having military training was great preparation for Andy to be in a relationship with me; he has a strong constitution and will endure hardship much easier than most.

As we approached the two-year mark of being together, I decided that it was time to take the relationship to the next level. When dating in my late thirties, using the word "boyfriend" seemed too high school and not to be tied to a serious, mature relationship. Besides, I wanted to make sure that I wasn't wasting what could be my last "marketable years" on a relationship that had no future, and I certainly wasn't going to be one of those women who wait five to seven years for a proposal that may never come. I mean, I'm Asian, and I'm adopted, so I had no idea on what day I'd wake up and suddenly be an old Asian lady with gray hair and a pruned face. ***My marketability clock was ticking, but I couldn't tell time.***

"I don't understand what the rush is," he kept saying.

"Because at this age and this far into our relationship, I think you should know whether or not you see this relationship going the distance," I argued.

I distinctly remember the conversation that I had psyched myself up for where I would give him the ultimatum. It was late in the summer of 2020, and Andy was outside doing yard work as I marched out to bring it up one last time.

"I just don't understand why you need to rush me. Maybe I can get you a promise ring," he tried.

"What do you think this is, junior high?!" I freaked out.

"I don't understand why we need to get engaged when I wouldn't be moving here until I retire in six years," he said calmly.

I tried to make my I-hate-the-word-boyfriend argument, but his rebuttal was, "I like calling you my 'girlfriend,' it makes me feel younger."

For real?

Well, as most things have gone in our relationship, he finally came around, and we got engaged. Did I see it coming? Of course, I had a photographer waiting in the wings. Since I knew I wanted to get married in the fall, I told Andy I wanted to get what I was calling "pre-wedding wedding photos" taken.

"We are only going to get older and less attractive before the wedding, and I don't want the stress of having a photographer at the wedding because I want it to be small and not cost a fortune, so if we get our photos taken two years before, it'll solve all of those problems," I explained in the most rational tone that I could muster.

"No," he said.

NO?! He didn't tell me no. At the time, I worked in a senior care facility, and I explained to him that people at the end of their lives only have photos to look back on, and that's all I wanted: photos. After a little crying on my part, he gave in. I got in touch with the photographer, and we were on his calendar two weeks later for a photoshoot in my yard, where the wedding would take place two years later.

Ordering white dresses, a brooch bouquet, pocket squares, finding alterations, and finalizing poses all in a few weeks' time was making me more insane than I usually am. The day came, and it all went great. "How did you feel about taking the pre-wedding wedding photos?" I asked him.

"I was like a zebra getting eaten by a lion. I just tried to look away and think of something else while it was happening," he responded.

After I had achieved the milestone I needed, I again tried to revisit the moving-to-be-together-sooner conversation. He would be moving to be with me eventually, so maybe he would reconsider now that we were engaged.

"No."

No again? What was happening?! I heard his reasons, but I didn't feel like he had considered ALL the facts, so I contacted the local police department's hiring lieutenant and set up a lunch meeting for the three of us. (Hubby's a cop, by the way, and he looks darn good in that uniform!)

"If, after this meeting, you still do not want to transfer to the local police department, I will stop trying to convince you that you need to move before you retire," I explained.

Well, he still told me no after the meeting, but at least I knew why, and that it didn't make financial sense for him to transfer, so I dropped it.

During this time of still struggling to be okay with the problems plaguing long-distance relationships, I asked the husband of a married couple "his opinion."

"Wouldn't you suffer the distance for the love of your life?"

Expecting him to respond like everyone else did, I was horrified to hear him too quickly respond, "No," as his wife stood beside him. Hmmm . . . I didn't understand his reasoning then, and I don't understand it now, so I brought the question to my in-house relationship translator, Andy.

He: When anyone says anything about not wanting to do something in a relationship when they redline, "I'm not going to do this, and I'm not going compromise on that," I don't think that they can conceptualize what a positive and happy relationship looks like. If you could visualize it, and you could look back and say, "Wow! This is what it's going to be like?" then his answer would have been different. Being in a positive and happy relationship can almost be compared to heaven. You have no perception of what that will be like, but we all assume that it will be so much better than we can imagine.

When you get to that point in a relationship and feel that way, you realize that things like distance are not hard to deal with at all. Nothing that comes up on the way to getting there is hard to deal with because your happiness suppresses and overcomes the obstacles. The enjoyment that you get from being in that amazing place elevates you to the point where you can do anything.

It's like love conquers all.

That's what you feel like when you're in that situation. It's not just an initial lust, and it's an actual tangible thing that you can see working on a daily basis.

She: Your saying "love conquers all" is a little bit fru fru fairytale for you.

He: Well, at the same time, with past trauma and things that I have seen and observed, I never saw a working relationship other than the one my parents had. I don't think you can really conceptualize how great it can be when all you've experienced is relationships that just don't work.

She: So, the person who told me that he wouldn't do a long-distance relationship for the love of his life, you don't think he found that connection with his current partner?

He: Definitely that, but I also think that he has no idea what you're talking about. Unless you've felt it, there would be no way of knowing. Long distance isn't what anyone wants to do because it isn't easy, but once you're on the top of the mountain looking down, you think, "that wasn't that big of a deal" because it isn't really. When you find your niche, everything just seems so easy.

She: But how do you describe that feeling to someone who doesn't know what it's like?

He: You can compare it to the initial honeymoon phase where you feel like the other person is the most amazing person ever. If you could think about that honeymoon phase being forever, that's what it feels like.

She: Is that where you're at?

He: Well, yeah. I don't have any complaints. The whole beginning of our relationship was like that for me. That testing, and waiting, and thinking, "Yeah, this will get old." I said something like that the other day . . .

She: Said what? To me?

He: You said something the other day about the five-year mark.

She: YOU said the five-year mark!

He: That's what I'm saying. When I brought up the five-year mark, that's still one of the tests I have in my psyche.

She: Is it a test for me, or is it a test for you?

He: It's a test for me. It's one of the walls I have up because of my history of relationships failing at the five-year mark when I started to feel comfortable enough to be myself. In those other relationships at that milestone, it wasn't me that broke them up. It was the other person. That failure happening over and over again screwed with my theory that if you love someone enough, it will always work out. The only way that loving someone enough that it will always work out can happen is if someone loves you the same amount.

Did my stoic, hard-exterior husband say the phrase "love conquers all" and compare our relationship to heaven? *Who is this man?!*

Obviously, he is being truthful when he responds, "I love you more," when I say, "I love you."

Oh my gosh, I'm the one that sucks a little more in our relationship! I hate that, but at the same time, I love it because it helps me understand how lucky I am.

As I look back on them, those few years between the engagement and our wedding didn't seem to fly by. Even after we got married, we decided that it still didn't make any sense for him to transfer to the local PD to finish his last few years of work. At this point in our lives, with a little less than three years left to serve of our long-distance sentence, it doesn't seem that bad anymore. Why?

I've become very independent, and that's a great thing. Because our relationship has always been long-distance and successful, I don't know it in any other capacity. It became our normal, and we adapted. We are certainly looking forward to living together full-time, and I know my boys are too, but that change will add a new element of learning and compromise to our relationship. The good news is, at that point, our love will have grown even deeper, and making those compromises will be nothing more than little bumps in the road.

Chapter 3: What is Love?

SHE SAID

Love is such a confusing word in its simplicity. We throw it around like it's such an easy feeling to generate out of thin air with statements like "I just LOVE this outfit!" Whenever Andy hears me say I love something, he responds, "Why don't you marry it?" Well, because I'm married to you, you goof. *Sometimes, he can be so childish, but he always makes me laugh.*

Truthfully, though, there is no more complicated word in the English language than the word "love." The Greeks were right to have different words for the distinctive kinds of love because the love you have for your family is SO not the same love you have for your partner.

How can you know with certainty that you are in love with someone if you don't know what being in love actually feels like? That is my issue with romantic love. How can you know what you don't know? Is the average person supposed to know if they are simply infatuated with someone or if they're in love? What's the difference? Is love a badge you earn after being infatuated with someone for a certain length of time? "It must be love since they've been together for two years."

Who is the final authority on the subject? The badge givers?

In this day and age of social media, impersonal relationships, and the degradation of in-person connections, some people think that love is when the other person takes a half second out of their day to change their social media status to "in a relationship." Even better, some people claim to know it's true love, and that they've found their soulmate if that person also changes their profile picture to a couples selfie. ***Stop kidding yourself if you are nodding and agreeing; social media has done love no favors.***

If we can't look to social media for the answers to life's mysteries, how about Hollywood? Certainly, the entertainment makers must know since we all keep buying into the Hollywood version of love. I think I've seen almost every romantic comedy ever, and for a long time, I craved that warm and fuzzy high that you get from watching the main character confess his love to the woman he can't live without. "I can't wait to have that perfect fairytale life," I used to tell myself in college as I sat in an estrogen-saturated room full of all women who were watching a chick flick.

That dopamine rush that we feel as the music swells is such a fleeting moment in time. That can't be what love is supposed to feel like, can it? Can you imagine having that feeling 24/7? It would be worse than pregnancy brain, and it's not realistic. Okay, so now where does that leave us? We could ask friends and family what love is. Ask the people who have surely lived enough of life and have been in relationships long enough to have earned the love badge. "You'll just know when you know," they say.

How is that helpful? Oh, and if these people are so in love, why do they seem to fight all the time or seem to roll their eyes when the other isn't looking? Is that the love we are all searching for? Someone we hate less than we hate everyone else? Someone we can cohabitate with and not kill? That can't be right. See, I told you love is complicated.

Let me explain how I came to understand what love is. I remember vividly one evening spent with a good friend as she was helping me with a project. It was a long, mindless task, and over several hours, she reminisced about her journey to love. Hearing how she described feeling about meeting her husband and hearing the passion and depth of emotion in her voice as she talked made me realize that I had not experienced that same feeling. What an odd epiphany to have over a decade into my first marriage. I sadly confessed to my very good friend, "I don't think that I know that feeling, and I don't know if I ever will."

I think that if you yourself have never experienced real love, being in the presence of someone who has and hearing it in their own words is as close as you'll come to finding it yourself. So, how did I get from not knowing to being this book's authority on love? The abbreviated version is simple. Divorce. I'm not saying that this is the path that everyone needs to take to find love, but it was mine, and it wasn't easy.

After about two months of dating Andy, I knew he was the one. I knew he'd be my next husband, and I knew that I loved him. I had never been so sure of anything in my life and finally figured out what everyone was talking about: I knew what I was supposed to know because I felt it with absolute certainty. He. Was. It. Granted, it took him twice as long to come to the same conclusion, but at least he got there. Almost exactly four months from the day we matched online, I was walking away from his house to my car, and I heard him say, "I love you."

Stunned, I whipped around and asked, "What did you say?"

"You heard me," he responded.

Finally. I had known for months that I loved him, and keeping it sucked in almost caused me to explode. My theory about who should say those three words first is that if I were to say it first, how would I ever know if he felt it or if he said what he thought I wanted to hear . . . and so, I waited. What did I do on my two-and-a-half-hour drive back home to my house? Like a true psycho, I called him and asked way too many questions about why he said he loved me.

"You're making it weird," he said matter-of-factly.

I know; I couldn't help myself. *I overthink everything.*

Fast forward five years, and here we still are, married on the fourth anniversary of the date that we matched online and had our first conversation, and we passed our first wedding anniversary. Cleverly, I planned our wedding on our anniversary so he would only have to hold on to one date in his slippery brain. I'm no dummy. Plus, I'm terrible with dates, so it's easier and more efficient this way for the both of us.

Some may say that five years is not enough to earn the "love of my life" badge. Here's the funny thing about taking love to the "of my life" status. Because I simply move at a much faster pace than most people, I knew within the first year that he was the love of my life, and so it was written into my wedding vows. A few years back, I asked Andy outright if I was the love of his life . . . I'm pretty sure we were engaged at that point. "No. How would I know if you were the love of my life if I haven't lived my whole life yet?" he retorted.

What a strange answer. I told you he wasn't normal.

One evening about a month ago, while my boys were at their dad's house, I had made supper for the two of us: nachos. I'm very accommodating to anyone in my home regarding food, so each of our sides of the sheet pan was tailored to our flavor sensibilities. I plated his food and served it to him, and I went back for mine. As I was sitting down, I asked, "Why aren't you eating?"

"I'm waiting for the love of my life," he said softly.

No way! He said it. What did I do? I made it weird again and asked too many irrelevant questions about what had changed. *I am human . . . and a girl, but at least I'm consistent in my weirdness.*

Anyway, the moral of the story is real love feels different. It feels comfortable, like your favorite loungewear, and warm, like getting into a bubble bath. It's an excitement that fades in and out but never disappears. It's looking at that other person and feeling like YOU'RE the lucky one. It is wanting to put that person's happiness above your own, no matter how selfish you are. It is not being able to be close enough to that person even when you're touching, or it's missing them when you're one floor away in the same house.

It's immediately wanting to say you're sorry when you step out of line because you know the other person didn't deserve it. It is making the other person's happiness a priority over your own. It's letting go of the other person's flaws and seeing past them to the heart of who they are. It's a peace that only your soul can identify as home, and it IS true: you WILL know what love is because that feeling is unlike anything else you will ever experience. Ever.

HE SAID

She: How would you define love?

He: It's security and freedom in the knowledge that you can be yourself and will be accepted for that. You don't need to keep your guard up, you don't have to worry about the other person and what they're doing, and you just know that they're there. They're going to let you be who you want to be, and you're going to let them be who they want to be. That's basically it.

She: What about thinking of love as a feeling?

He: It's a chemical reaction. If you're trying to define it, there are other ways to define it. Imagine love and happiness in a relationship like an empty bucket that you share with your partner. The sand is love and happiness, and the empty space is resentment and unhappiness. With each good deed done for the other person, a little sand gets scooped into the bucket. The fuller the bucket becomes, the less and less space there is for resentment and unhappiness. If each person is contributing sand to the bucket, it fills faster. Growing in love is a team effort.

She: How do you KNOW?

He: I think most people know right away.

She: Like within the first five minutes of meeting someone?

He: No, in the first short period of time . . . I don't ever second guess myself about you; that doesn't ever come up. But I remember being in relationships where I quickly started second guessing myself like, "This isn't that good," or "Maybe I could find better than this." I could simplify it, but it makes me sound animalistic. If I don't find you appealing naked or if I can see down the road that this person isn't going to have the longevity to keep me interested, then I start to peter out. I'm not going to put any more work into the relationship, and usually, if I haven't ended it, I'm going to frickin' start sabotaging it so it does end on its own.

She: So, do you think love is all that complicated?

He: It doesn't have to be. It's as complicated as you make it. I don't think it's complicated at all.

Most men and women identify love very differently. Women feel loved when they feel cherished. Men feel loved when they feel respected. For me, love is a feeling . . . a very intense emotion that becomes a steady but comfortable warmth. My sweet husband dismisses love as a chemical released by your brain, and he simplifies it down to what's important for him to be in love: someone letting him be himself and still loving him. I suppose that at the root of a successful relationship, acceptance is key.

If he didn't accept my intense Type A personality, or if he was trying to change me constantly, I'm sure that we wouldn't find ourselves mutually happy in love in our relationship. Love can feel like or be something different for every person, but what I am certain of is that whatever it looks or feels like, every person knows when they're in love.

HE ASKED

1. What are three things that would be better in your life if you were in love?

2. Does your answer include "I wouldn't be lonely anymore," "I would finally be happy," or "Now I'm not the only one who doesn't have someone"? If so, then you may be looking to use love as a band-aid to fix problems in your life that cannot permanently be fixed by love, and you should be asking, "Why do I feel like I need to be in love to be happy?"

Chapter 4: Attraction and Relationships

SHE SAID

Let me start by admitting to you that this chapter has been the most difficult chapter to write and rewrite and rewrite again. The topic has been controversial and has been referred to by some to be borderline offensive. I have wrestled with the content of this chapter for days through feelings of guilt and through several heated discussions with my husband about what should and should not be written.

Struggling with not wanting to lose my voice or my opinion while also trying to find a way to convey the information in a way that is more inspiring than controversial, I want you to know that it is not my intention to offend anyone with the narrative that you are about to read. I feel like sometimes we need to hear things that make us uncomfortable for us to push ourselves to be better.

If you were to meet me right now at this juncture in my life, you wouldn't believe that I ever felt unattractive, not confident, and fat. Throughout grade school, I was a shy wallflower that no one noticed or wanted to date. I felt plain, I didn't know how to dress for my body type, I didn't know how to style my Korean hair, and I didn't know how to put makeup on because I was one of two

Koreans in a small town of mostly Caucasians. All I ever wanted as a child was to be like everyone else with blonde hair and blue eyes.

When I went to college, I told myself it was my chance to reinvent who I was (essentially to suck less) without the shadow of my whole shy childhood sneaking around behind me. During my first year of college, I watched boy after boy after boy make attempts to woo my roommate. She was one of the pretty, popular people in high school. She was everything that I wasn't. She was effortlessly confident, and I studied her, trying to figure out what it was that made boys so attracted to her.

On Valentine's Day in my first year of college, I remember her getting roses from three different guys while I sat boyfriendless and flowerless. The college I went to had a ratio of about two girls for every one boy, and she was taking three boys.

My very first boyfriend was one that I met in college because we were friends. A year or so into our relationship, I asked him if it made him at all uncomfortable that I was Asian because he was white. Not helping my backlogged issues of insecurity about being different, he said, yes, it did bother him a little bit.

When I turned twenty-one, I met the man who became my first husband. And while our marriage did come to an end, I have him to thank for helping me to realize the beauty of being different and to embrace my Asian appearance. That shift, however, was only part of what made me the confident person I am today.

Throughout my whole life up until several years into my marriage, I hated the thought of regular exercise. I wanted to want to do it, but I just couldn't find the internal strength and motivation to do it. I hated running, even though I tried several times to like it.

Four years into my too-comfortable marriage, I found myself fifteen pounds heavier, and I didn't like how I was starting to look in pictures. Over the Thanksgiving weekend of 2008, we took a trip to Arizona to celebrate with my ex-husband's family. His older sister, who is ten years older than I am, had everything that I thought I wanted, AND she was super fit and super attractive.

One afternoon, when everyone else attended a basketball game, she took me shopping at a mall where I could afford nothing, and the one thing that I did want to buy, I was going to have to buy in a size that I never had to buy before. I remember that moment vividly. It was embarrassing, but it was important to the change I decided to make shortly thereafter.

After shopping, she and I met one of her friends for lunch. As she and her co-Barbie friend chatted, all I could think about was how uncomfortable I was because I felt like the ugly, fat one at the table who wasn't good enough to be included in the Barbie Dreamhouse conversation.

I sat there thinking, "If she can look like that, and she's ten years older than I am, so can I!"

It was time to suck less at feeling like I did and how I felt about myself.

As soon as I got back home after that trip, I got on the treadmill twice a day and dropped those fifteen pounds in a couple of months. Ever since that traumatic event, I have made fitness a priority in my life, even through two pregnancies. Even though my motivation at the time stemmed from a different place than it does now, I tell you these painful truths about my past to let you know that it is possible to take control and change things if it's something that you really want to do. I did it; it was and is not easy by any means, but it is possible.

> Jane thought her husband Dick was a solid ten in attractiveness when they met and married, and while he continued to stay fit and well-groomed, she found herself less and less attracted to him. He had stopped bringing her flowers and had started making excuses not to help with the children or household chores. Making matters worse, he never made time to take her out for a date night once in a while.
>
> What happened? He was still "attractive" in the physical sense. What happened was she lost respect for him. In losing respect, she lost patience and started to communicate through nagging and yelling. Her lack of attraction to him in their marriage led to less and less intimacy in their relationship, and that left Dick unhappy as well, so he continued to pull away and was less and less inclined to even consider doing anything nice for Jane, let alone go above and beyond to help her out.

Into the marriage quagmire, they tumbled. In Jane's unhappiness, she found herself putting less and less effort into her appearance; she turned to emotional eating, and her style seemed to be more sweatpants and messy buns than put-together outfits. Dick found himself even more miserable and unattracted to the woman he once thought to be the most beautiful woman he'd ever seen. Her constant nagging, combined with the lack of intimacy, made her more and more unattractive to him.

They both started to wonder what happened to the spark they once shared, the laughter that used to happen so easily, and the intimacy that used to be effortless. They were both sucking, and they needed to find a way to suck less.

Because I know how much work it takes for me to stay in shape when I was looking for husband number two, I was looking for someone who shared my internal desire for fitness, health, and, yes, appearance. In our relationship, Andy and I put a lot of value in the effort that the other is putting in to maintain attractiveness in our relationship, and for us, it is important to try to maintain the level of attractiveness that brought us together.

I love that I don't have to beg him to exercise, and I know for a fact that he feels the same way. I am admittedly a bit extreme in the things that I do when it comes to exercise every single morning, dying my hair to get rid of the gray every two weeks, putting on a full face of makeup every day regardless of what I'm doing, and wearing stilettos any time I leave the house.

A lot of the reasons that I put so much effort into how I look stem from some sort of trauma. I used to hate it when people or little children would stare at me in my hometown because I was different. As I got older, I decided that I wanted to control the reason people looked at me, and now, when they do, I tell myself that the reason is how I dress or how I look. I never leave the house without being all done up, and I try every day to be as attractive as I can be. It is a lot less painful for me to think that now the reason people stare at me is that I'm attractive, not because I don't fit in.

I am not suggesting that you go to the extreme measures that I do. I have issues, clearly. All I'm trying to express is that if you are serious about being successful in relationships, it would be helpful to your cause to put in a little extra effort. A little extra effort could mean something as simple as changing out of your sweatpants and putting on regular pants or a dress when you leave the house. It could be introducing some sort of exercise into your week, even if it's only thirty minutes one day a week. The important thing is that you are trying and putting forth effort to better yourself physically, mentally, or even in your career, and that effort is attractive.

One wonders, if attraction isn't important, why do fitness centers, personal trainers, fad diets, or even Snapchat filters exist? I feel like society is sending mixed messages in wanting everyone to feel happy with exactly how they are while simultaneously advertising for us to look better with this exercise or that face cream. According to Alliedmarketresearch.com, "the global skincare market size was valued at $146.7 billion in 2021," and according to Helplama.com, "the beauty industry's net worth is estimated at $579.22 billion in 2023" (M and V 2023, Helplama 2023). Whether we like it or not, the physical is clearly valued by some people if those industries are grossing so much profit.

Neither my husband nor I are suggesting that in order to find love, everyone has to look like a supermodel. In being the way that we are and sharing our story and our thoughts, we are trying to inspire and motivate you to get what you want when it comes to love. When it comes to fitness or matters regarding appearance, I'm still not exactly sure what it is that differentiates inspirational people from the people others want to run after with pitchforks. However, as I stated at the beginning of this book, I am not the kind of friend who tells you what you want to hear. I'm the friend who tells you the truth, encourages you along the way, and becomes a cheerleader for your success.

> *When Jane eased up on nagging Dick, his attitude toward her warmed again, and he arranged a date night. Before the date, she got her hair and nails done, she looked for an outfit that made her feel pretty, and she set aside her comfy sweatpants for the evening. Because Dick showed her how he was committed to their marriage by making plans for a date, she started treating him with more respect, and the cycle continued toward a more positive mutual attraction.*

HE SAID

She: Do you think that attraction is important in a long-term relationship?

He: Yes. Super important.

She: Does how smart, how funny, or how much a woman makes have any influence on how attractive you find her? Why or why not?

He: Funny is the only one that would have any kind of benefit. Actually, how much money they make is the least qualifying factor for attractiveness. It's nice, but it's not that important to attractiveness; it's not even something I look at. Yeah, smarts, I don't care about that either because someone can always get smarter.

She: That's not true.

He: Someone can always get smarter, funnier, or make more money, but they can't get better lookin'.

She: (*Laughing*) With makeup or plastic surgery, they could.

He: Nah, not very easily.

She: What role does attractiveness play in the health of a long-term relationship?

He: What? Isn't that the same question?

She: No, what role does it play as something goes on for a long period of time?

He: It helps maintain respect between the parties involved. I need the person I'm with to put in as much work as I am. I know what kind of work it takes to keep myself in shape, and if you're doing the same thing to keep yourself in shape, then there's mutual respect there. If one of the parties drops off in effort, then there's a tendency to lose respect and desire. You always want to have a desire for the person you're with.

If I'm not attracted to somebody later in a relationship, I'm not going to want to be with them. It also depends on what you tie to attractiveness, though. If you start tying other things to attractiveness, like how the person acts or how much they contribute to the relationship, then that could detract from their overall attractiveness anyway. You can be with someone who's super attractive, but they can become unattractive when you get upset with them. I've lost attractiveness for people I thought I was in love with.

She: Because of what?

He: Because of the way I thought they treated people, but for the most part, they just stopped being as attractive as they were when I met them.

She: Have you been in a relationship where someone started to let themselves go? People can be attracted to each other going into a relationship, and everybody puts so much effort in to hook somebody and get them to be committed, but then they get so comfortable...

He: DO THEY put a lot of work in though?

She: Most people put more work into the beginning than they do later because . . .

He: Yeah, there's that five-year mark when people start to let themselves go . . .

She: Oh! Like right where we are now! (*Laughing*) What do you think about people making excuses like, "I don't have time . . ."

He: Excuses are just that, excuses.

She: What about when women say, "Oh, he'll still love me after I gain a few after we get married because he fell in love with what's on the inside and who I am as a person."

He: I think it's naïve. Everyone should be comfortable in the knowledge that their partner will stay around in a committed relationship, but I always made a big deal to people up front that I want them to be and stay attractive because that's important to me. It's been important from the day I met you. I always want to be attracted to you, and some of that attraction will become stronger as you get older because of shared experiences, but you still need to maintain a standard.

Do I really want to sit on a beach somewhere with someone that looks totally unattractive? No, I don't want to do that. Had you not been the way that you are with exercise, makeup, multiple showers a day, and putting so much work into how you look every day, maybe I wouldn't have stuck around . . . I don't know.

Attraction is a very big part of your draw to each other, and when people don't find each other attractive, it affects how you're wired to be intimate.

She: Okay, stop. You're getting into the next chapter's topic.

Regardless of how anyone interprets it, this information is based on my and my husband's personal experience. I completely understand that no one wants to hear that they may have to put in a little more effort that will add one more thing to an already busy day, but this is self-help advice that can be taken or left. However, when it comes to making any changes in your life, you "Gotta wanna," as my dad used to tell me when I was a kid. I never understood what he meant until I got older and started to understand how important internal motivation is when it comes to achieving your goals.

If you have even the slightest inkling you want to put more effort into your appearance, you want to feel more confident, or you're currently unsatisfied with how you look, I can relate. I felt that for the first twenty-one years of my life, but I did find a way to change it. If you are happy with yourself just the way you are, good for you! You found what it took me a long time to find. Happiness with yourself will outwardly show in how confident you are, and I'm pretty sure that confidence is universally attractive.

My hubby and I both agree that when it comes to attraction in long-term relationships, both parties should always be trying to maintain at least some of the attraction that brought you together. That could apply to physical attractiveness, attraction to personality traits, or even attraction to strength of character. One would hope that the things that brought you together would be an important factor in what keeps you together and happy.

HE ASKED

1. Is having a physical connection with your partner important?
2. If your answer to #1 is "yes," then do you currently have a good physical connection with your partner?
3. If your answer to #2 is "no," then why do you think that is?

Chapter 5: What Kind of Intimacy Currency Is in Your Wallet?

SHE SAID

When I was online dating before I met my first husband, I went on a few dates with this guy who was super nice and polite, but every date was awkward. His profile photo was taken from a mile away, and I think it was also an old picture. And while he tried so hard, it simply wasn't there. On our first date, we met at a restaurant, and he brought a dozen roses. "What's the special occasion?" the server asked excitedly.

"First date," I muttered, embarrassed enough for us both.

I mean, the guy was really nice, so I thought maybe if I give it one more shot, things might turn around. Nope. Just more awkwardness. So, I did what most people would do at that point: I asked if he wanted to be friends. I hated it. I felt so bad, but you can't make yourself feel something that doesn't happen naturally.

Passion is instinctual. It's primal. It's evoked from somewhere we can't control with our minds, and that's why attraction is important and can't be overlooked. You can't force passion to happen just because someone seems like they should be a great fit for you. If it's not there, it's simply not there. There's no sizzle.

Some people equate intimacy with sex, but it is more than that. Let's face it: sex is one of the big three issues that couples fight about. Why? The reason is that typically, women are only in the mood when they feel appreciated, loved, taken care of, and cherished. When women respect their partners, they are also much more likely to want to be intimate. I have a great deal of respect for my husband, but he also makes me feel cherished and appreciated.

Respect + Love + Being Cherished = a great ongoing bedroom chemistry.

I believe that good intimacy in a relationship is necessary for warm fuzzies to be shared between partners. The problem is, how can intimacy be a good, shared experience if one party isn't ever in the mood? Do you have any idea how many times I've heard of women withholding sex in a relationship to manipulate their partners? That's such unhealthy behavior, and I admit I have done it in the past, and I'm not proud of it. At the time, however, I didn't understand the right approach to get what I needed.

Andy says that men express love through intimacy, and intimacy to men means sex. They need it to feel connected to their partners. For each party in the relationship to have healthy intimacy, both parties must get what they need and give what their partner needs.

> *Dick and Jane had this same intimacy problem. The problem they have is with the currency they are trying to exchange. Dick's*

intimacy currency is the Yen (sex). He needs his currency to be accepted by Jane for him to be happy. Jane's intimate currency is the Euro (help with the kids and chores), and for her to exchange currency with Dick, she needs him to accept her Euros. Dick keeps trying to hand Jane Yen. She keeps asking him for Euros, but he has none.

Finally, they realize they need to find a currency exchange to convert their differing forms of currency, and they find one at Dick and Jane's Bank of Intimacy. At the bank, Dick trades in his Yen for Euros, he pays Jane with Euros, and she accepts the currency. Jane brings her Euros to the bank, exchanges them for Yen, and gives Dick his preferred intimate currency and fair trades are flowing effortlessly.

The more Dick and Jane's Bank of Intimacy was used the way it was intended, the more successful it became. The exchanges got easier and became habitual, and their Bank of Intimacy was successful.

Intimacy in relationships can be easily set aside as a bonus because so many other things seem like larger fires that need addressing first, and life can simply be exhausting. I'll admit that sometimes I'm too tired or too stressed to put intimacy at the forefront of my mind. While I enjoy the intimacy in my relationship immensely, I sometimes find myself sucking at initiating when I have a lot on my mind. However, I do understand how important it is to the health of my relationship, so I have made a silent promise never to deny intimacy when it is initiated.

My husband and I have found that the keys to successful intimacy are as follows:

1. Maintain attraction.
2. Find a way for both parties to get what they need and want.
3. Make sure you make time for that physical bonding exercise.
4. Splitting initiation 50/50 helps both parties feel like intimacy is a priority to the relationship's health, and it helps both parties feel attractive, desired, and loved.

Non-sexual intimacy can also be vital. Sometimes, people can find satisfaction in physical intimacy with their partners in other ways than just fun in the bedroom. Personally, I love a good snuggle nap on the couch. There is something about how my left cheek lines up with his bicep as I'm tucked under his arm that instantly puts me to sleep. It's one of my favorite things, rare as it happens because my house is often chaotic and loud.

Sometimes, Andy will take my face gently in his hands and kiss me softly. It's also one of my favorite things, but it doesn't happen often either. My favorite form of non-sexual intimacy is when I'm 75 percent asleep in bed, and I can feel him softly touching me or holding me tightly, but I'm too tired to wake up or say anything. It's not at all sexual in intention or expectation . . . it's a much deeper intimate feeling than that. The haze of not being asleep or awake puts an ethereal glow around the warmth of simply being cherished. That's my favorite.

I know I'm a lucky girl in all forms of physical intimacy with my hubby. While I do savor every moment of the non-sexual physical intimacy in my marriage, the sex is also out-of-this-world fantastic. I think in Andy's dating profile, he said something about being a "snuggling grand master" or something like that, and it wasn't a made-up selling point. With how differently people can be wired, intimacy can mean something different for everyone, but fulfilling intimacy can only be checked off the relationship goals box if both partners are getting what they need in order to want to be intimate. Being successful in intimacy is a major win in a relationship because that means that most everything else is going well, and intimacy is the warm, fuzzy cherry on top.

HE SAID

She: How do you define intimacy?

He: There could be a lot of definitions: there's the intimacy that involves telling someone all your secrets or allowing them access to your bank account, and there's physical intimacy.

She: Is that what intimacy means to you? Sharing a bank account?

He: Well, yeah, I suppose. I don't do that with anybody else.

She: We don't share a bank account.

He: I know, but information-wise, you were able to access my account, go through it, and see what I spent my money on. That's pretty intimate. I would also say that intimacy reflects vulnerability. Some people give out physical and emotional intimacy easier than others. Even a one-night stand has a degree of intimacy that's shared, and once you've given away that level of intimacy, you can't take it back.

She: What does physical intimacy in a relationship look like to you?

He: Bumping uglies . . . sex, holding hands, all that stuff. There's usually an aura of intimacy around couples who are in that healthy intimacy bubble together; they're communicating with their energy, and others can sense it.

She: What is the key to good intimacy?

He: Communication. If you don't share with someone what you need, how can they provide what you need? People need to communicate their definition of intimacy to each other. You can't assume that your version of intimacy is the other person's version.

So, apparently, my husband is a deeper thinker than I am when defining intimacy. Who knew that sharing banking information could be intimate? He keeps me guessing, which I love. We do, however, agree that intimacy in the bedroom is extremely important to the health of a relationship.

If you ever ask someone who is in a miserable relationship about their sex life, it's either terrible or nonexistent or a complete chore.

I have a friend who went a year without sex with her husband right before she filed for divorce, and I have another friend who cried into her pillow during sex in her short-lived marriage. Some women don't actively participate or initiate physical intimacy unless their needs are being met by a partner who understands what they need to be happy.

Intimacy is the indicator of the health of a relationship, like a canary is the indicator of the health of a mineshaft work environment. If the canary goes in and comes back sick, there may be ways to make that environment hospitable to work in. If the canary dies, all work stops. If intimacy dies, the relationship is doomed. Don't let your intimacy canary die—you may not be able to resuscitate it after it goes brain dead.

HE ASKED

1. As the manager of your Bank of Intimacy, what can you do to make sure that the exchange rate is fair for both parties involved?

2. How do you incentivize making deposits into your bank of intimacy a priority?

3. How do you tell customers how they can avoid high interest rates or fees at your Bank of Intimacy?

Chapter 6: Trying to Change Him Will Make You Miserable

SHE SAID

Have you ever slid into a relationship with someone with flaws you knew would be an issue, but you convinced yourself that you could fix him, change him, or ignore his flaws? I have. Sometimes, in times of desperation, we overlook things because that person has potential or is oh-so-close to what we want. As time passes, we try and try and try to change those little things, all while growing increasingly frustrated, angry, and resentful that things aren't being changed to our liking.

As I tend to do with most lessons that life is trying to teach me, I learned the hard way that you cannot change someone. Believe me, I tried. It is impossible unless someone gets a lobotomy or amnesia and forgets everything about who they used to be. Just the urge to try to change someone is a warning sign of failure down the line . . . the timing of said failure depends on how long you can stomach dealing with the things you want to change but will never be able to.

How can you avoid this relationship chasm? Counseling? Maybe, but it didn't work for me.

In an ideal situation, if you want to avoid the pitfalls of trying to fix someone, you would take a break from dating and relationships, make sure you've healed and are confident in who you are, and then use my Three-List Method.

The first list you must make is **The Must-Haves**, the deal breakers. The must-have list should be a short list of up to five or six items. These dealbreakers are the biggies like religion, politics, kids, finances, etc. Try to keep this list short, or you may price yourself out of the market by being too picky.

The second list is **The Must-Not-Haves,** which can also be deal breakers if they DO have these. For instance, things on my must-not-have list would be smoking and wanting more kids. I'm not having more kids, and I can't stand smoking. Dating a man who was perfect in every other aspect but expected joint children or who smoked would be a stupid waste of time. Inefficient. Be careful not to make this list too long if you've been unsuccessfully dating for a long time. Step back and think about what you cannot deal with . . . also around five or six items. We want this person to exist in real life.

The third and final list is **The Nice-to-Haves**. While somewhat important, this list isn't the final say. This list aims to help you understand what you want and are looking for. Hair color, geographic location, career, hobbies . . . These are all things that could be on your nice-to-have list. I mean, someone may put having a six-pack on this list, but how many men will pass the first two lists and have washboard abs? See what I mean? These items may help you narrow your search, especially if you're online dating or asking friends and family for assistance in finding love.

The key to finding success in the Three-List Method is to make these lists in a completely neutral relationship mindset. Dating or shopping for dates will skew your data and cloud your judgment. I've seen this phenomenon happen. Someone will be shopping the online man catalog while making her lists, and she'll find herself making concessions, "Well, he's cute and successful . . . I can overlook the smoking issue." Or some women fresh out of a bad relationship will put all their past partner's flaws on this list.

I've sucked royally at trying to change someone in two separate long-term relationships, but I have also done my homework and made the lists after those experiences. While recently trying to tell a friend about the Three-List Method, I went home and pulled out the list I made before meeting my current hubby. I was curious to revisit the list and compare Andy to it. Sure enough, he checks all of my must-haves and most of my nice-to-haves, and he does not have any of my must-not-haves. Making lists helps you take a step away from emotional decisions and moves decision-making into the realm of rationality. When it comes to something as emotionally driven as relationships, sometimes we need an exercise in rationality, especially if you are making the same mistakes over and over as I have.

People are so emotionally and visually driven that mixing dating and list-making will only put you on a path to nowhere, and at the end of that path, you'll simply be less marketable to your target audience. Another important factor in the Three-List Method is that you need self-respect. Without self-respect, you may self-deprecate when you meet someone who's either missing something significant on your Must-Have list or who has something from your Must-Not-Have list. Many women who don't respect themselves or value themselves will talk themselves into not being worth the man configured from the lists, and then they will settle for something that will inevitably fail.

> *When Dick and Jane went to buy their starter home, they had a long list of must-haves along with an idealized perspective of what their new home would look like. However, the more homes they looked at, the more they became confused about what features were must-haves and which were nice-to-haves. The confused couple became pickier and pickier and thought everything was a must-have. The problem was that they couldn't afford everything on their revised must-have list.*
>
> *When they had to take a step back and break down their list into the must-haves, must-not-haves, and nice-to-haves that would align with their budget, they were finally able to find a home that matched their needs and their budget.*

Like Dick and Jane's home-buying process, the more people you date, the pickier you can become. While the lists of must-haves and must-not-haves are important, so is being realistic. If you can figure out the equation that balances what you're offering with what you can expect, you're on the right path. What happens next? After you've figured out the lists with realistic expectations, you can go into the dating world knowing what you want and what won't work.

Having these standards makes dating more efficient. You won't waste time with people you know will not work long-term. I have had friends fall into the trap of not doing the work upfront and failing, and failing, and failing, and failing, and then finding themselves significantly more unmarketable and emotionally damaged before they realize they had been going about it all wrong.

One of my friends who recently got married is constantly bothered by the fact that her husband smokes.

"Did he smoke when you met him?" I asked her.

"Well, yes," she responded.

"Well, then you can't get mad at him for being the same person that he was when you met and chose him," I rationalized.

The way someone is when you meet them is their free pass to continuing to be the same person with the same behaviors and characteristics for the duration of the relationship. Thinking he's going to change is on you. That's your bad. And thinking that he should be someone other than who he started out as is you sucking a little.

I have been in relationships where I have tried to make him value exercise, tried to make him want to be more driven in a career, tried to make him more expressive about his emotions, tried to make him stop treating me like a child, tried to make him drink and swear less, and the list goes on and on. Not once in these relationships did trying my darndest to change them work. For all my efforts, I was the only one left frustrated and annoyed. Change simply wasn't something that was going to happen because I wanted it to, and I was sucking because I thought that I could change someone from who they were when I met them.

Going into my relationship with my hubby, I knew what I wanted and what I didn't. When I was looking for a house after my divorce, I only looked at one house because I knew what I needed, didn't need, and would like to have. Yes, I sat down one day and typed up my lists for finding that home like I did for finding my current husband. Making the lists helped me to be very efficient in looking for another partner, and it did not take long for me to realize that Andy was it—he was my list in the flesh.

I know my Andy isn't perfect . . . he's human. Here's the thing, though: his flaws are not things that will drive me insane. I know I can't change him, and I don't try. However, he can be led to adjust small behaviors with the right approach. Approaching your partner in the moment when you're angry and upset is NOT the way anyone, husband, child, or pet will respond in a positive manner.

Let me share with you the socks-in-the-laundry story. I do all the laundry in the household . . . it's fine because I assigned this chore to myself. Whenever I did any laundry, I would find his black socks in balls. When I pulled his socks out to their normal elongated shape, they would neither be clean nor dry. I'm such a stickler for efficiency, and having two small items dirty and wet after the whole laundry cycle had been completed made me furious. Way more furious than socks should make a rational person. Did I want to freak out at him about the socks? Of course, I did. Did I? No, no, I did not. The reason I tried to change my own instinctive reaction is that I love him, and he's a good husband. He didn't deserve that kind of childish reaction.

Good husbands make good wives who want to be the best versions of themselves. I took the sock, walked slowly over to my husband, held out my hand, and gave him the sock. "Would you fix this sock, please? Whenever you put balled-up socks in the laundry, they don't get clean or dry. It would make doing the laundry so much easier if you would fix the socks before you put them in the laundry. Would you please try to remember to fix them?" I asked.

Did this calm interaction change his behavior immediately? No. But I kept repeating this same calm request with the same hands-on teaching method. The first time I noticed the socks in the laundry pulled out as I had requested, I made sure to let him know that I noticed and appreciated his extra effort and the fact that he listened. Over two years after the initial sock conversation, I have not had the balled-up sock issue. He was retrained.

But you said you can't change someone! I know. There's a difference between changing someone's core personality and learning to cohabitate harmoniously with another person. The keys to making successful adjustments, like with the socks, are mutual respect, a calm demeanor, repetition, and reward.

While this kind of repetitive teaching may seem like a great deal of effort, once you have found a method that works for both of you, you can use the same method to make any further adjustments. When you have established a pattern of success, you will reach a higher level of respectful communication.

HE SAID

She: Have you ever been in a relationship and tried to change someone?

He: (*Pauses*) No. I don't think I've ever done that. Even in relationships that weren't working, I haven't tried to change the other person. If something wasn't working, it was usually a physical incompatibility.

She: Have you ever been in a relationship where someone was trying to change you?

He: Every single one.

She: What did they want to change?

He: (*Sighing*) They wanted me to focus more, they wanted me to be more responsible, they wanted me to be more intuitive to what they were doing, they wanted me to communicate better. They just wanted me to do better, and I just wasn't able to do it.

She: How did it make you feel when you realized they were trying to change you?

He: It's a bad feeling because it makes you feel like you're not good enough, or you think that you're wired wrong and that you're broken. It shouldn't be like that; you should feel accepted for the person you are. After so many breakups, I started to realize that there wasn't something wrong with me. The problem was that I was picking the wrong people who wanted to fix or change me.

Some of the things they wanted to change, I would have changed on my own, but I would have needed the proper motivation. It's unfortunate that most people don't see it that way. Instead of trying to fix someone, you should be supporting them. If you support someone in the direction you want them to go, they'll go that way.

She: Did you try to change when people in past relationships wanted you to?

He: I tried because I wanted to make them happy, but they expected the change to happen overnight. I was taught to believe that if you love someone enough, they'll love you back, but if someone is trying to change you, you're just not with the right person. Instead of trying to change someone, you need to pick someone better from the beginning, but most people don't have the fortitude to hold out and put the work into finding the right fit.

She: Was anyone successful in changing you?

He: Yeah. They changed me for the worse. Let's say at the beginning of the relationship you have a lot of confidence, but then the person you're with starts picking at you: "You're driving wrong," "You're eating wrong." The nitpicking wears away your confidence in yourself, and then you start thinking you can't do anything right.

You then carry that hurt into your next relationship. You try to be someone you're not because the last person didn't like who you were, and then you just start a cycle of picking people who are not a good fit for you. Others see your vulnerability, and they see someone they can manipulate to fit their ideal of what they want. The more that cycle is allowed to continue, the more you lose your identity and become an angry person with walls up. You try to sabotage any subsequent relationships because you're so screwed up in regard to what you want and what people want from you.

If you don't repair that damage and just keep jumping into the next relationship, it will tear you apart.

She: So, the only kind of change that someone can get out of their partner is negative?

He: No, if you support your partner, it's different. Trying to change someone and trying to support someone to be better are two different things, and I don't think that everybody knows that. Most people use negative reinforcement or punishment to try to change a partner.

She: What amount of change do you think is reasonable in a long-term relationship? Like why did you change how you put your socks in the laundry?

He: I changed that behavior because I could see the logic in doing it that way, and it's such an easy thing to do. Out of every hundred socks, if I miss one or two, I don't get yelled at. If someone is just unhappy about something bigger in the relationship, it comes out as nitpicking the other person about little things. Everything their partner does becomes a problem.

She: What general advice would you give women who are trying to change their partners?

He: Start out with one thing you want to change and support your partner in the change. Until he's at a point where he can maintain that change himself, don't start trying to change anything else about him. Also, don't expect the change to be done to the degree you want. Understand that any amount of change in the right direction is a big deal and a manifestation of how much he cares about you.

Before you make any sort of commitment to someone, like moving in together or getting married, you need to look at the other person's past behavior in instances when you tried to get them to give you what you need. If you find yourself having the same argument over and over and nothing changes, or you've asked them to do something over and over and nothing changes, that person is clearly not a good long-term fit for you because they didn't care enough to even try. If that happens, it's time to move on.

Going into a relationship with someone whose flaws you know will bother you down the line is a road to nowhere. While changing someone should not be your top priority, if you want to see some small adjustments from your partner, you should approach it like you would trying to teach your children something. You don't give your child one chance to learn or change a behavior, and if they don't do it right away and to your satisfaction, you put them up for adoption.

If we accept that parent-child behavior pattern as normal, then why are we so unwilling to put that same investment of time toward the goal of a successful, happy relationship? As parents, we treat our children with unconditional love. That depth of love is patient and forgiving, so why can't we treat our partners with the same patience and forgiveness? Positive reinforcement in any relationship, even in work relationships, is the best way to try to encourage change.

If you can treat your partner with supportive, unconditional love, he will be inspired to be better and do better. That adage of wanting to be with someone who makes you want to be a better person really is true. The adage isn't "I want to be with someone who yells at me to change and slowly steals all of my self-confidence."

If your partner even meets you halfway, like in negotiating the purchase price of a home, you should be happy with any amount given in your direction. Most people don't get everything they want all the time. The bottom line is that you cannot change someone. Please stop trying. It hurts them and makes you angry, resentful, frustrated, and exhausted. Find someone whose flaws you can love, treat them with patience and grace, and suck less when you're working together as a team to make little compromises.

If you find yourself single, don't see that as a negative. It's a great place to be to set yourself up for success if you do your Three-List Method homework. Sit down with your favorite comfort beverage of choice, a notebook, and a pen that makes writing enjoyable, and make the lists. You will look back and be thankful for the time and effort that you invested into the happiness of your future relationships.

HE ASKED

1. Why would you expect a relationship to be successful if you don't even know what you want or need to have a successful relationship?
2. How long are you willing to be unhappy before you do something about it?
3. Would you want someone to try to change you to suit their needs to be happy in the relationship?

Chapter 7: Men Are Inherently Lazy

SHE SAID

Andy says that men in relationships are inherently lazy; however, men are only as lazy as they are allowed to be.

"Laziness is a little harsh," Andy recanted when discussing this topic with me. "Men can easily become comfortable and begin to take things for granted, which can come across as laziness," he elaborated.

> *Jane thinks that Dick is lazy because he always seems to be taking naps in the middle of the day while she is busy cleaning, cooking, and helping their kids with homework. "I'm just resting my eyes," explains Dick as he eases into his recliner and kicks back to relax.*
>
> *"No, you're taking a nap!" she yells in frustration. In her heightened state of annoyance, Jane stomps away, making as much passive-aggressive noise as she can with the dishes and the vacuum and doing anything else she can to make Dick's nap less productive and less enjoyable.*
>
> *Further exacerbating her annoyance, Dick happily snores away. All Jane wants is for Dick to ask her, "Jane, is there something that I can do to help you?" but she's sure that if she ever heard him utter those words, she would die of shock.*

My Andy takes naps, but he earns them. Naps used to be a point of contention in my other relationships, but even though Andy takes a lot of naps, I find myself covering him with more blankets, turning the lights off, and trying to be as quiet as I can be. Why has my reaction changed so drastically when it comes to napping?

The reason is that my hubby does ask if there's anything he can do to help me, especially when he can tell I'm getting stressed out and overwhelmed. He's a quiet observer, and that's one of the things I love most about him. I always make "Hubby to Do" lists for him, and as long as he completes his list in a timely fashion, I couldn't care less how many naps he takes.

> *Since Jane thinks Dick has too much free time because he's using it to take naps, she has asked him to help out more. However, when Dick does help, he doesn't complete the task to the level that Jane would, so she ends up doing it again and then not asking in the future. The cycle just starts over, and she starts to wonder if Dick intentionally screws up tasks on purpose so as not to be asked again for help.*

I have struggled with the same issue that Jane has when redoing a task that I've asked Andy to do. From day one, when Andy was at my house, I asked him to make the bed after he got out of it. It only makes sense for the last person out to make the bed, no? I like to get into a well-made bed at the end of the day, and he has made the bed every morning he's been here, but his version of making the bed and mine are two different things. For a while, after he made the bed, I would simply upgrade his bed-making to my standard. I was torn between taking over the task or simply letting him continue to do it poorly.

It makes no sense to have two people do the same chore right after each other. It's inefficient. In my first marriage, I made the mistake of taking something over so that it was done right, but in doing that, I took on way too many of the household chores, and I became resentful. What to do, what to do? As calmly as I could muster, I told Andy, "I appreciate that you made the bed, but weren't you in the military? Don't you have to pull the sheets tight enough to bounce a quarter off them? Do you think that you could try to make the bed a little neater?" Okay, it was a little snarky, but it was the best I could do. I am still trying to suck less when it comes to NOT using a tone with my husband.

Did he do better? Yes, yes, he did. There's no punishment or reward system here. Getting help from your partner is often about how you approach them and the health of your relationship. If you're not on good terms with your partner, you can ask or yell all you want, but you won't get help.

Here's the thing, though: if you don't ask for help and start taking over everything so it's done to your standard, your partner will likely sit back and let you take over. It's not just husbands. Most people work this way. If you never had a review at work, goals you had to meet, or a boss who kept you accountable, would you try very hard at your job? No. The key to getting the help you need is communicating respectfully. If you suddenly snap when you're overwhelmed and tired and start yelling at your partner, "Why can't you help out more?!" you've shot yourself in the foot.

In Dick and Jane's case of perceived imbalance of effort, they both need to suck less. Jane needs to suck less at how she communicates, and Dick needs to suck less at the timeliness and quality of the chores he's been asked to do.

HE SAID

She: You've said to me that when you see the trash or recycling by the back door, you just take it out. What motivates you to do those things without being asked to do it?

He: I want to be good energy in our relationship. I'm putting deposits in our bank of trust. You have to do things and build up a consistency of showing you're reliable. If I do these little things, I know there will be a reward.

She: So, you're building up your points bank?

He: Yes, but it also helps you teach yourself good behavior. If you knock out your little tasks quickly and on a consistent basis, it teaches your brain to work that way. I know if I train myself to do the things that I'm asked to do over and over, if I make a mistake like forgetting to fix a sock before it goes in the laundry, that mistake will get overlooked.

Once you've trained yourself, the other person will notice and will think very positively about you, minimizing smaller conflicts.

She: What motivates you to want to retrain yourself?

He: I can see the value in going above and beyond what I'm used to doing or what I want to do because I might get a big reward down the line. That makes sense to me; I'm smart enough to figure that out. In turn, if I see the other person doing a lot of things for me, like making me breakfast in the morning, or making sure my shirts are always folded so they look nice, or the house is always clean, then I feel like I should be doing something equal to that effort because I don't want to do that stuff.

By not taking the trash out, what benefit am I really getting?

She: You don't have to do it. That's what you're getting.

He: But it only takes a few seconds, and what did it cost me? I know that if I don't keep doing things without being asked, I won't get what I want. If I don't take the trash out but turn around and expect sex in the middle of the night but don't get it, was it worth not doing that little chore only to be denied what I want? No.

She: Why do you think so many men struggle with doing what they're being asked to do?

He: There haven't been any consequences. Many women will not hold their partners to a standard that was set or established. "In the beginning, this is how you were; what's changed?" "Why are you not doing it anymore?" "If you're not going to do it anymore, then we're done." In other words, you need to address any change for the worse right then and there, and you need to follow through.

This is the first relationship I've been in that's successful, so these things must be working. When I slip up, you address it right away, and it keeps things balanced, but most people do not address issues right away, and they don't do it calmly.

She: Have you always been this willingly helpful in past relationships? Why or why not?

He: No, I wasn't for years and years, but there's a maturity aspect now. At the beginning of a relationship, a woman may be singing your praises. Whether or not you dismiss them, those kinds of compliments and ego-boosters make your partner feel like a man and feel strong, and men want to keep having those feelings. I think a man needs a cheerleader to push and inspire him.

Women should just accept the fact that they're going to have to put more work into the relationship than the man. If a woman asks her partner five times to do something, and he only does it once, then why would she keep trying the same approach? She needs to try something different that gets better results.

Women need to understand that their partners can't read their minds and won't do things exactly like they would. Men don't do things the way women want them to, not because they don't care about their spouses. They just don't think the same way. When I was in the military, I did well because someone was always checking on me and holding me to a standard. I need to be supervised, and I need to be with someone who is willing to tell me what to do. I can do things if I'm held to a standard, but the moment you stop telling me to do things, they won't get done.

While I would never characterize my husband as lazy, he's the one who calls himself out on it frequently. The funny thing is that when he says he is, I argue that he isn't.

Andy usually has a good amount built up in his spousal points bank, so I do give him free passes on little things, like when he left his post-run sweaty towel on the sofa. "He's a good husband, he's a good husband, he's a good husband," I chanted silently to myself as I cautiously picked up the moist, stinky towel and walked it at arm's length to the washing machine.

And yes, he earns the bedroom privileges in the middle of the night, even though I value my sleep and will be a witch if I don't get an uninterrupted 7.5 hours.

Maybe the perception of laziness simply comes down to a mismatch of expectations based on life experience and how people were reared. However, if you can set clear expectations and timelines and ease up when they're complete, you won't end up with a partner who doesn't help. He has his part to play too, but if both parties work together to divide the work equally and suck less, everyone will be happier and less exhausted.

HE ASKED

1. Is it reasonable to think that different people will come together in a relationship with different expectations on the state of the household based on past experience or the environment they grew up in?

2. Knowing that a little encouragement might lead to a willingness to do more, do you think it's valuable to give credit to your partner even though your level of expectation isn't being met?

3. Can you separate these gaps in expectations from being a personal attack on you? If you know your partner loves you and isn't doing things a certain way just to annoy you, can you understand that fact and let your differences go?

Chapter 8: Set Expectations Up Front

SHE SAID

After having to start over after my fourteen-year marriage, I was determined to do everything possible not to make the same mistakes that I may have made the first time around. After all, marriages don't usually end because of only one person. Sometimes things just don't work out because people don't want the same things out of life, or they got married before they knew who they were and what they wanted, or one wanted kids, and the other didn't . . . or any number of things that aren't only one person's fault. If a relationship ends, that doesn't mean either person is bad. They simply didn't align.

While I may not have known who I was or what I needed when I married the first time, I was positive that if I ever got married again, I was going to do as much research as I could to avoid another failed marriage in the future. Type A's hate failure . . . Well, at least I do.

In doing my research, I learned that knowing yourself is one of the first steps to being successful in any relationship. I know that I will take over tasks if they aren't done quickly enough or to my standard, so I needed to suck less at creating my own relationship issues. I had been letting my partner off the hook while enabling him to be less helpful when all I wanted was help. Sometimes I can be my own worst enemy, but I'm always working on finding ways to suck less.

> *Jane is a control freak. She had a really hard time not taking over tasks, but she knew she needed to figure out a way to ask Dick for help, encourage him to keep helping, and learn to let go of little things. "That's so much easier said than done," she thought. Jane had previously been in a relationship where she felt like she did 99 percent of everything while her partner complained that he was so sick of hearing that she was so tired all the time. "Of course, I'm tired all the time," Jane cried to her best friend. "I'm just exhausted, and I feel like Dick doesn't appreciate me or all that I do."*

The first weekend Andy and I met, the weekend my husband seems to recall much differently than I do, I cooked for him.

However, I remember saying, "I think it's fair if I cook, you do the dishes, don't you?"

Affable as he is, he agreed and has since been jumping up to do the dishes as soon as the first person is done eating, which, ironically, is him. However, just like with the bed-making, the way he was loading the dishwasher and putting dishes away was starting to annoy me because he wasn't doing it like I would.

Granted, the man had never had a dishwasher, so how could I expect him to know how to load one? Still . . . I can't stand inefficiency. I would reorganize the dishwasher after he'd loaded it because I didn't want him to stop doing it. I worried that if I corrected how he loaded the dishwasher, I would run the risk of his not continuing to participate in the chore. Knowing what I know now, I wish someone had informed me that men are very simple when it comes to communication, and I should just express verbatim what I want instead of running scenarios in my head.

Eventually, I calmly talked with him about how to load the dishwasher properly, what could go in, and what needed hand washing. The putting away of items in the wrong place was tricky. While I appreciated his blind efforts at putting things away regardless of whether they made it to their correct destination when he would leave to drive back to his house, I would find myself searching for ten minutes for the spatula I wanted. Then I would call him to ask where it was, but he wouldn't remember. The whole cycle seemed counterproductive.

When Andy isn't at my house, and my youngest son is, it's the youngest's job to empty the dishwasher. He is the only other person in the house (not his older brother and not Andy) who knows where everything goes. If he does not know where something goes, he puts the misfit items on the corner of the kitchen island. Sometimes, he organizes the spoons or makes tall structures of the leftover items he doesn't know where they go. It's cute. It's efficient, which is the way I like it. I have caught him correcting Andy on where things go. He's so my kid.

Jane became so frustrated with Dick that she started to think of him as another child to take care of. However, in comparing him to their children, she realized that she could use the lessons learned from being a parent and apply them to communicating effectively with Dick.

Jane decided that instead of pointing out the mistakes that Dick made completing the chore he was asked to help with, she changed her approach and spoke more softly and sweetly to him like she would if she were trying to teach their child something. What happened? Dick felt like he was helping, and he felt appreciated because he was no longer getting yelled at for doing something wrong. Finally, Jane was content with the division of chores because he was trying, and she was less exhausted. A relationship gold star for Dick and Jane!

Sometimes, it's the smallest things that our partner can do for us that mean so much and show us how much we are loved. My weeknight evenings are tightly structured: dinner promptly at 5:00 pm, cleanup, 6:20 snack time, 7:20 teeth brushing, 7:45 kids read in their rooms and put themselves to sleep, and our short window to relax when the kids are in bed. For some reason, the dishwasher always sends its annoying "I'm done" beep right when I sit down to relax. It never fails. The dishwasher is my relaxation nemesis.

I'm up at 4:00 am every weekday morning so I can work out, primp, and get the kids and myself off to where we need to be. I don't sit down at the end of the day until I'm done with everything because I know that if I do, I won't get back up. Right at my most tired moment of the day, after I've gotten comfortable on the couch, the dishwasher screams at me from across the room, "Oh no, you don't! You're not done with chores, silly. Walk your tired butt over here, open the door, and turn me off. You know I won't stop intermittently beeping until you do." This dishwasher is a nag. It does NOT stop beeping until you get up and turn it off. I assume that at some point in the middle of the night, it eventually gives up, but it's long after I'm asleep.

My attentive husband has taken it upon himself to leap up at the sound of the first beep, walk over to the evil dishwasher, and turn it off. Seriously though, that's my real-life version of a knight in shining armor saving me from the evil dragon. Dishwasher, thy name is Dragon. He knows the beeping bugs me, and he knows I'm exhausted. He loves me enough to want to help me regardless of how tired he is, and I love him for it. It's such a little thing, but it is in the little things where love grows deeper.

As far as setting expectations on the bigger concepts of labor, we divided the outdoor vs. indoor chores early on in our relationship. Andy and I are old-fashioned when it comes to traditional gender roles as they define women's work and men's work. I'm fine with our arrangement because I know my partner is doing his share when he's here at my house. He has never asked me to mow, and this last record-setting snowfall winter, when the mall's roof collapsed under the weight of the snow, he told me he would take care of the snow on the roof of my garage. That day, he got up at 3:00 am, worked out, worked a shift from 7:00 am until 5:00 pm, and then drove two hours north to my house. The moment he arrived, he got out the ladder and a shovel and climbed up to the garage roof to start shoveling in the dark. He's my hero. Looking at him, I visualize his metaphorical superhero cape flying behind him. Andy always tells me that when I talk about him to others, I must make him seem better than he is, but my response is, "Isn't that a good thing that I see you that way?"

The next morning, after Andy tried to rescue the garage roof from collapse, I called the whole family to the rooftops to shovel. It was an emergency. All four of us worked for hours clearing the roof of the garage and shed. Andy kept repeating to me, "You don't have to do this. I don't want you to get hurt. Take a break." It was my own stubbornness and quest for more exercise that kept me up there. I hated that winter, and I was going to kick it off my roof. I did, however, love him more each time he told me he would take care of it because I know he would rather hurt or exhaust himself than ever wish that upon me. Gallantry can also be heroic; there is far too little of it anymore.

> *When Jane started to acknowledge that Dick had completed a task, any task, she made sure to tell him that she appreciated what he had done and praised him for his good work. While Dick never asked for any thank yous, the positive feedback that she provided him was*

appreciated in his own way, and their relationship started to repair itself and grow deeper.

While setting expectations and sharing the workload is important, it is equally important to acknowledge your partner's role and accomplishments. I know that Andy would rather I compliment him by saying how great the yard looks than compliment him on how he looks. In turn, he knows that I need to feel appreciated by being thanked for any meal I make and serve him, and I like him to notice how much effort I put into how I look.

Most evenings, we sit down to dinner, and before he lifts his fork, he says, "Thank you for dinner."

Between you and me, I think he says it at the front end of eating so that he doesn't forget.

When he's up doing the dishes, I kiss him and say, "Thank you for doing the dishes." On the rare occasion when he forgets to thank me for dinner, when he's doing the dishes, I lean over in front of his face, kiss him, and sweetly say, "You're welcome for dinner." Which is followed by, "Oh, thank you for dinner..." and then the thanking for the dishes and so on.

Just because something is expected or understood does NOT mean that gratefulness should be forgotten. If I kept doing my tasks, and he kept doing his, and neither of us acknowledged the other's hard work, resentment would still find a way to seep into the relationship. Expectations, equal division of labor, and gratitude are all imperative to setting a relationship up for success from the very beginning.

For people already deep into a relationship, you can work together to reset expectations, divide the chores, and implement gratitude. Still, it will be exponentially harder for you to break established behavior patterns and retrain your brain. It's not impossible, but it will be very hard work. If you think that your relationship and your partner are worth the hard work, you should definitely try to make the changes necessary to bring peace and appreciation back into your relationship.

HE SAID

She: What did you think that first weekend we spent together when I said that if I make dinner, I'd like you to do the dishes?

He: I'm easygoing, so I did it. Who would say, "No, I'm not doing that!"?

She: I thought you'd have a deeper insight into it like, "If I do this now, I'm going to have to keep doing it."

He: No. I frickin' said that in the beginning, I'll do whatever it takes to get what I want.

She: Do you remember my asking you to make the bed that first weekend because I like to get into a made bed at the end of the day?

He: What did I just say? I would have done a lot of things that you asked me to that weekend.

She: How do you feel about our traditional gender role views on division of labor: like you do the outside stuff, and I do the inside stuff?

He: I'm cool with it; I don't like doing inside stuff, but I would do it if I had to.

She: Has it always been that way in your past relationships, or did you think someone ended up doing more than 50 percent of the work?

He: It's pretty much always been that way, I think.

She: In all of your other relationships, did you usually have those gender-defined roles?

He: I don't remember.

She: You're not being very helpful.

He: You're asking about things I haven't done for six years.

She: You should still be able to remember!

He: I can't remember my name half the time.

She: UGH! Does it bother you that I don't mow when you're gone?

He: No, not at all.

She: Have you been in relationships where you did what you were asked to do, or you did something consistently to help, but the other person never seemed grateful?

He: Oh yes! That was a huge issue in the past.

She: Did their ungratefulness make you stop helping?

He: No. It just added more crap to the crap.

She: Can you articulate that a little bit differently?

He: You just feel disrespected, I guess. You just don't feel like you're appreciated. Those are things that come up in arguments, "I do all this stuff, and no one appreciates it."

She: So, you keep that on your mental scorecard. Is that what you're saying?

He: Yeah, but I'm not vindictive like that. I could see how other people could be. You're only going to put up with that behavior for so long before you start getting crabby.

She: Do you think that people in relationships where one person is doing significantly more of the work can find a way to rebalance the work mid-relationship?

He: Not without some kind of therapy. They may be able to do it for a little bit, but unless you have people who are very disciplined, it's not going to happen.

She: How do you think that a balance of 50/50 labor can be achieved in a relationship?

He: I suppose lists might help; there would have to be some kind of structure to it so they can see exactly what is expected.

She: Well, the chapter is about setting expectations upfront.

He: Well, yeah, if you're able to do that, but most people date for so long that by the time they cohabitate, they've already established a lot of bad communication habits. It's also easy to get defensive when someone brings up a conversation about dividing chores mid-relationship. If you do that, you'll get a response like, "Well, I'm doing just as much as you are!"

•——·

All is NOT fair in love and chores, or as Andy calls it, "Chorin'." He's from Iowa. Andy and I are in total agreement that the best approach to achieving an equal division of labor is setting those precedents and expectations at or near the very beginning of a relationship. You don't have to do an inside/outside division like we do, but you need to make sure that both parties feel like there is a fair split.

If you are in a relationship with patterns already established, good or bad, both of you will need to work very hard to suck less and to find ways to change your habits and how you communicate with each other. It will not be easy, and you may need to seek third-party help, but creating an environment where everyone feels like a team working together will pay off for your relationship.

HE ASKED

1. Is it important to have boundaries in a relationship?
2. If you think boundaries are important, are you mentally and emotionally healthy enough to adhere to your boundaries and respect those of your partner?

Chapter 9: Actions Will Show You His True Feelings

SHE SAID

Have you ever been in a relationship where a man tells you that he loves you, but you are conflicted because how he acts and how he treats you doesn't seem to match up with the words he's professing to you? Have you ever had promises made to you in a relationship, only for those promises never to be turned into actions?

I have, and for your sake, I hope that hasn't happened to you. In all reality, however, it's easy to fall for the lip service a man is love-bombing you with because of our inherent need to feel desired and loved. For you to be able to step back and analyze whether or not your partner's actions are aligning with his words, you would need to be able to separate your emotions from your logical brain, and that's so much easier said than done.

> *Jane was in a lip service type of relationship like this before she met Dick. Adam was her first serious boyfriend. In the first few weeks of their relationship, Adam showered her with compliments, flowers, attention, and dinners out. He even initiated defining the relationship as boyfriend and girlfriend. She was hooked. "He must really be into me," she told her bestie.*

A few months in, however, Adam seemed to be giving her the words she wanted to hear to keep her invested in the relationship, but he wasn't making time for her, he wasn't calling her, and he didn't seem to be showing her that she was a priority in his life. "I don't understand. He says he loves me and is lucky to have me, but he never seems to have time for me," she complained.

"I'm sorry to tell you this, but I don't think he's all that into you," her bestie responded with empathy.

"But he still texts me in the morning, and he still refers to me as 'baby,' and he still has the picture of us together as his Facebook profile picture," Jane argued.

Poor Jane. She wanted to be in a loving relationship so much that she just couldn't step back and look at the situation logically. Logic would tell her that if he isn't backing up his words with actions, he's not all in. Jane's emotions were overpowering her logic, and she just couldn't see the hard truth. It was time to end it. He was quietly quitting their relationship by slowly distancing himself, but he was also putting the ball in her court so that he wouldn't have to be the bad guy and initiate a breakup.

When her best friend's words of logic finally sunk in, Jane broke it off in a text. Adam's response was, "I figured." He knew the game was over because he had stopped playing to win. Adam got his drama-free pass out of a relationship that he just wasn't into anymore, and Jane was left to reevaluate and start over.

In relationships, it is the actual doing and long-term consistency that lets you know someone's level of love and commitment. From his actions, I knew early on that my Andy was committed to our relationship because he drove back and forth in our long-distance relationship. For five years, he has been driving the two hours to my house from work and the two-and-a-half hours back to his house, and he will continue his love pilgrimages for three more years until he retires, sells his house and moves in with me. No one would put that many miles on for that many years if it was only a booty call. I know because I asked him once in our first year of dating,

The more I learn about love, the more I wonder, do most women even know what they want from a man? It sure took me a while to figure it out, and romcoms and fairytales were certainly no help. I used to devour rom-coms like a cake put in front of a person who had been intermittently fasting. I'm so hungry right now, and I love cake so much.

Popular culture puts so much emphasis on needing to hear "I love you" from a partner like it's the unscalable mountain that we must conquer to be happy. In romcoms, the profession of love is usually accompanied by some grand romantic gesture.

In that equation, they are right. Words must be joined at the hip with actions to equal true feelings.

But why would a man tell us he loves us if it isn't true?

"Men will say anything to women to get what they want," Andy has told me many times, even though it took me years to believe it could be true. "Men should just say 'I love you' back when a woman says it first, even if the man doesn't feel it because even if he said he loves her, he can still leave and say he doesn't love her anymore. She wouldn't ever know if he told the truth or not."

I know it sounds bad, but it's the truth straight from a man who has played the game and gotten what he wanted.

> *Jane's truth in her situation with Adam was that she was sucking a little at choosing the right partner, holding him to the standard she needed and that he provided at the beginning of the relationship, and staying in it too long after his words stopped aligning with his actions. When she finally came around and ended the relationship, she learned from her mistake, and she sucked less at love. Then she made her three lists, and she went out and got Dick. Good for you, Jane!*

I know that my hubby loves me to his core. How can I be sure of that fact? Because he tells me, and he shows me. The man shows me more than he tells me, and I prefer it that way. Sure, when I say, "I love you," he replies robotically, "I love you more." Do you, though? "Prove it," I challenged him once on a long road trip. We had stopped at a gas station, and being the candy connoisseur that he is, his treat from the pit stop was bottle caps. Before his door closed, those bottle caps were savagely torn into. Being of the mindset that what's yours is mine and what's mine is mine, I kept holding out my hand for the cola-flavored pieces.

"This is how much I love you," he pointed out. "I love candy, and I love bottle caps. My favorite flavor is the cola ones, and I'm giving them all to you."

That little sugar-coated gesture, insignificant as it may seem to an outsider, was a big deal.

Andy is a man of action, and I've had to learn that about him over time. That's how he shows his partner love. In the deadpan way that he speaks, it's hard to believe him 100 percent when he tells me how he feels, so it's good that he's a man of action. To his credit, Andy does spoil me with handwritten sweet nothings in cards or the occasional poem as a gift, but 95 percent of the time, he's what my best friend refers to as "The Liquid Terminator" who moves quietly in the shadows without much emotion or words.

So, what does my robot husband do that I interpret as love? Whenever I ask him to do something, he does it, and he does it without delay, without grumbling, and without irritation. He's a man of his word. I remember one day when I was mad at him about something (obviously, it was a huge issue because I can't remember why I was mad at him that day), and I was primed to pick a fight with him. As I heard him pull into the garage, I looked out the bedroom window down to where I could see him walking from the garage to the house. I was ablaze with fury. Ooh, he would get it from me when I got downstairs!

Wait. What was that he had in his hand? I knew he'd gone out for a car part for a project that annoyed me to no end, but that telltale red plastic spoon standing upright in a colorful cup filled with something sure looked like the indicator of my favorite blended ice cream treat. Racing down the stairs to the back door, I felt my annoyance evaporate as he presented me with a cotton candy blizzard. What car repair project? Anyone who knows me knows that I hate surprises, but treats and flowers I'll take any day, and I do.

On another occasion, I recall being annoyed at him for something little. Still, when I heard the back door open and that all-too-familiar crinkling noise of cellophane wrapped around a bouquet of flowers, all was forgotten. I can't remember why I was mad at him, so, clearly, I suck sometimes, and I know I suck at my petty snap reactions to little things, but I'm working on it.

These acts are manifestations of love because in neither instance was he bringing me something because he was in the doghouse. Like in most instances when he's in trouble, in these moments, he was blissfully unaware that the door to the doghouse had opened when he was out. Andy does these sweet things for me because that's one of the ways he expresses how much he loves me. Like I said, a doer, not a sayer, a man of action . . . which is fine because I talk enough for the both of us.

The fact is that both doing and saying are essential to feeling loved and cherished. If he truly loves you, he will show you and tell you. He will make compromises, consider your feelings when making decisions, want to make you smile, want to ease your burden and tell you that he loves you.

HE SAID

She: Do you think that when men say "I love you" they really mean it?

He: How would I know that?

She: Because you probably said it a lot. Did you always mean it?

He: No, I didn't always mean it, but as I've gotten older, now I only say it if I mean it. I do know people who say it to everybody pretty quickly, but if they mean it, it depends on what their definition of love is.

She: In all of your past relationships, have you ever said, "I love you," and not meant it?

He: Oh yeah, well, I said it thinking I meant it, but I didn't really mean it because that comes with a lot of things.

She: Like?

He: When you say it, you need to mean it. I've had people say they love me, but they don't mean it because of the way that they act.

She: If a woman can't rely on those three words to know if a man loves her, how can she know?

He: By how he treats her; that's the biggest thing. Women are always complaining about how their partners treat them, and that's a clear sign their partners obviously don't love them. A man wouldn't do so many things to upset you and he wouldn't be outright disrespectful if he really loved you.

She: What goes through your mind when you're out and about and make the decision to make an extra stop for my favorite blizzard or for flowers?

He: I just think, "Oh, it'd be nice to do that," or "I want to do this for her." It's easy to do, and it's something I can do in the moment.

She: But if you're out doing something like being out on a specific mission to get a tool, how do you transition from that into thinking, "Oh, I should probably do something for her" because most people don't do that?

He: If you love someone, they're on your mind a lot, even if you're focused on another task. Because we have a strong connection, I'll find myself thinking, "Oh, Cyndi would like to have that," when

I see things that you'd like. Doing those little things for you is easy for me to do, so I just choose to do it.

She: But it's a whole separate stop sometimes. It's not like you're already there.

He: Well, sometimes I just think, "I haven't done this for a while," so when I'm out and about, I'll do it, or I'll add it to my list for when I go out. Sometimes, it's spontaneous, and sometimes it's thought out.

She: Soooo some of it is premeditated, and some of it is spontaneous.

He: Yeah, you do those things when someone's on your mind all the time. It's just like with your kids when you think, "Oh, my kid would like this." When you love and care for someone like that, those thoughts just pop into your head.

She: But those thoughts don't cross a lot of people's minds when they're out and focused on other tasks.

He: That's the difference in the amount of passion you have for someone. When you build up good memories, good feelings, and good times with each other, and there's good communication and not much negativity, a big door opens that allows for those kinds of things to happen naturally. That brings me back to my point: If you harp on someone all the time, those little love gestures get pushed farther and farther out of your partner's mind. Why would you want to do something nice for someone if they're always mean to you?

If you want someone to do little nice things for you, you need to treat your partner well and do nice things for them, hoping to get some in return. If you're after someone all the time to do something like bring you flowers, you never give them the opportunity to do it on their own.

She: Why do you think that most men don't continue to come home with little surprises after they've been with someone for a long time?

He: People take each other for granted, and sometimes people get hung up in their lives . . . like people sometimes bring work issues home. You need to learn to separate your life and not take everything so seriously. I don't carry a lot of my work life with me, and it makes my personal life a lot easier, but I don't think a lot of people can do that. So many people are selfish and in their own heads that they aren't willing to put anyone else's feelings first.

When it comes to us, I want to be with you. When I'm gone, I'm not happy, and I'm excited to come back. When I'm in that happy mindset, that's when the thoughts about you are positive and inspire me to do things for you.

She: What advice would you give women who are being told they are loved but don't feel like they're being shown it?

He: You can confront your partner and cause it to be an issue, or you can change your behavior. "You seem like you're distant tonight. Did something happen today? Is there something I can do for you to make you feel better? Can I shoulder some of what you're going through?" Be supportive and . . .

She: So, you have to draw it out of them?

He: Maybe, but I think you have to do it in a way that isn't pushy; you need to create a situation where it could happen, but don't be forceful about it.

Sometimes, when it comes to love and relationships, you need to trust your gut because your gut is your logical brain fighting your emotional heart. While it's sometimes easy to take an antacid to quiet the rumblings of your gut, eventually, it may hurt so much that it cannot be ignored.

Real love in your relationship should inspire both of you to act in ways that show your partner how you feel. When those gestures of love become effortless for both parties, you will be able to feel the shift in the maturity and depth of love in your relationship.

HE ASKED

1. Are you willing to accept that from a man's point of view, words will tell you what he's thinking, but actions will show you what he's feeling?

2. If his words and actions aren't lining up, are you going to trust your gut that something just isn't right?

3. Do you honestly believe that little "e" efforts equal big "I love yous"?

Chapter 10: If You Keep Score, You'll Never Win

SHE SAID

When the new relationship smell wears off, one or both of you may question the relationship's equality. "I did this, so you should do that." "Who paid the last time for dinner, and does it equate to the last two times I paid for dinner?" "If he borrows my car, will he chip in for gas?" This line of internal questioning will inevitably lead to someone starting a mental scorekeeping checklist.

> "He left his crap on the table again!" complained Jane to her friend. "He left the TV on when he went out, and he tracked dirt onto my clean floors!" Jane continued on her rant about the list of things that Dick was doing to put himself deeper into the doghouse. "He's driving me nuts! He's so far in the doghouse that he can't even see the light of the opening."
>
> "Jane, it sounds like you're focusing on a lot of little things. Do you think that maybe there's a bigger problem in your marriage?" her friend asked.
>
> "I don't know, I'm just so frustrated," Jane responded.

Jane had started a scorecard and added at least three tick marks against Dick, and the marks were multiplying at an astonishing rate. Did Dick have a scorecard too? Did he even know that score was being taken? Likely no and no. I assume that women tend to be the scorekeepers because we are multi-thinkers. We may be completely busy with a task, but our minds are left free to overthink everything. I try to stay busy, but sometimes, I simply can't stop myself from obsessively ruminating.

Conversely to how I overthink and keep score, I have never heard Andy call me out on something that I did or didn't do. Never once has he taken something petty and held it over my head. Have you ever stopped to ask your partner what he's got on his scorecard against you? I did. I asked my love even though I was hesitant to hear his answers in case he told me that I sucked at something.

"Is there anything that I do that annoys you?" I asked because surely there had to be something he was holding on to but wasn't saying.

"No. Well, at least not that I can think of right now," he noted.

Why couldn't he come up with something? Am I completely without fault or flaws? No. He simply doesn't keep score, and he's happier for it. He does not dwell on the little details like I tend to do.

Sometimes, we can get so easily tripped up by things of little significance and then start making marks on our mental scorecards. Envision that with each tick mark made against your partner, you are taking a scoop of quicksand and dumping it right onto your path. The more tick marks you add to your scorecard, the deeper and deeper you end up sinking into a quicksand bog of your own making. Before you realize it, you have buried yourself alive, and it's too late. The relationship has been suffocated by all the things you were holding against your partner—petty little things they probably had no idea they were doing.

The unfortunate fact is that when we're young girls, we are given directions that lead us straight into a mire of relationship quicksand. We grow up witnessing so many women—friends, mothers, coworkers—all dive headfirst into the sinking sand. From a young age, our internal GPS is programmed to drive us straight into relationship death.

How can we redirect our GPS systems and set ourselves on the right path on the road trip of life? The best way to avoid driving straight into suffocation by quicksand is by being able to see the trap, reroute, and avoid it completely. My husband's and my advice can give you the right coordinates to plug into your GPS. No, I take that back. Our advice goes back to more traditional, stripped-back relationship thinking. We are the old-school paper map telling you something different than your new-fangled GPS.

When retraining your brain to forgive and forget the little annoyances or wiping the scorecard clean, try to remember that you're your own worst enemy in quicksand scorekeeping. This lesson is one I still struggle with. It's my immediate reaction to be annoyed at the little things and start talking to myself like a crazy person.

One morning, after Andy had left for the gym, I came downstairs and saw that he had left the back entry light on. My irritation button immediately tripped, and I found myself grumbling aloud to myself, "Seriously, Andrew Lewis? Didn't I just say how expensive my electric bill is?!" I tend to use full names when I'm angry. I'm not sure why because it's not like there was another person named Andy in the house at the time.

I had that scoop of quicksand in my hand, and I was about to dump it in front of me. Because I'm trying my best to be more emotionally aware and mature in my second marriage, I could talk myself into getting rid of the sand. By the time he got home, my irritation had dissipated. About an hour later, as we found ourselves in the car on our way to the beach, he told me that on his drive home from the gym, he was thinking to himself how lucky he was to have me. Oooh . . . Didn't I feel like the shitty, petty, score-keeping partner?

Now, imagine how differently things could have gone if, when he walked through the door, I came at him all angry and annoyed, "You didn't turn off the mudroom light! Don't you know how expensive my bills are?!" If I had done that, I certainly would have ruined his musings about feeling lucky in our relationship. Warm fuzzies instantly would have frozen into frigid icicles.

What would one vapid statement like that have done to the health of our relationship, and how much more work would it be to fix it? Tick marks are easy to put on a scorecard, but erasing them when you made them in permanent marker is not so easily done. What did I learn from that morning's interactions? I learned that I need to try to forgive and forget when it comes to the little things and throw away my scoop of scorecard quicksand. I needed to focus more on the larger things, like being grateful for having such a kind and wonderful partner. There was a moment of realization of knowing I needed to retrain my brain.

What I'm working on, and you can do it with me, is recognizing that bad behavior pattern and training my brain to think about something good that was done for me recently . . . like how he tries to refold the living room blankets, how I like them or how he takes care of an item on his to-do list and crosses it off. Let's start replacing the little bad thoughts with little good thoughts. Trade those scoops of quicksand for planks of wood that will help you cross over that relationship death trap. The quicker and easier that you can begin to make those trades, the easier it will be for you to breeze right over those traps of quicksand. Let's all try together to suck less.

HE SAID

She: Why do you think little things like leaving your stuff on the counter bug women so much?

He: Because other issues aren't being addressed, and those things are just symptoms of a bigger problem. If someone loves their partner and is happy with them, little things aren't a big deal — that stuff gets overlooked. However, if you're not getting your big needs met, the little things are intensified simply because you're unhappy. You'll pick on your partner for the little things, "Well, if he could just do these things, it wouldn't be so bad."

She: Do you think that women or men keep score more in relationships?

He: There's always going to be one person who puts more effort in than the other; that's just the way life is.

She: I'm not talking about putting effort in, I'm talking about keeping score like, "Well, you did this . . ."

He: I don't think people keep score until there's a problem.

She: So, they just pull a scorecard out of nowhere suddenly?

He: When someone is in an unhappy relationship, they can spew out a whole long list of complaints about their partner. If they were happy, there would be no need to keep score. Why would you do that? We don't keep score. People keep score so that they can tell their partner that they're not doing their share of the work. Am I wrong?

She: We're in a happy relationship, but sometimes I do it; I have to check myself.

He: Well, that could also be habitual if you've done that in past relationships or have seen it in your parents' relationships.

She: How have you felt when a woman has gotten angry at you for something unintentional like leaving on a light?

He: Depends on the situation. If it's not that big of a deal, I'll just take it. I don't care about that stuff, but if someone were doing it all the time for everything, it would get old. If it's only occasionally, people are human and will make mistakes, and I don't even think about it. If you care about someone, you don't have to feel attacked and defensive. You don't have a lot of negative feelings because there's no reason to have them.

If someone has a chip on their shoulder or has past trauma, they will point out little things that their partner is doing. If that happens, I always assume it's because they're mad at something else because I don't do things intentionally to hurt people.

She: What advice would you give couples to avoid the pitfalls of scorekeeping?

He: You have to be forgiving and understanding of people's moods and what's going on, and you also have to be conscientious that certain things upset certain people. If you know what those triggering things are and can understand why they would be upset about them, then you can put in extra effort not to do those things.

You can't be selfish and do whatever you want. For example, at work, when you know something bothers one of your coworkers, you don't do that around them. If your partner has too many of these little things they keep score about, then you need to look at your relationship to see if it makes sense and if that person is a good fit for you.

When you meet someone, and they are telling you what bothers them or what their overall preferences are, you'd better listen and identify if what their preferences are will be suited to how you are. The problem is that most people don't do that work up front; they take for granted that there will be work involved to make it successful.

Keeping a scorecard of your partner's flaws is a sure sign that something needs to change. Either you need to change your attitude, change how you communicate, or change partners. Pointing out every tiny mistake, holding grudges, and grumbling to yourself like a crazy person are all unhealthy behaviors.

Resentment formed from piles of scorecards will kill your relationship.

If you find yourself with a list of negatives longer than positives when it comes to your partner, your relationship is almost sunk in the sand. However, if you can recognize the problem before you suffocate, you can try to pull yourself out. With hard work, self-reflection, and forgiveness, eventually, you'll be able to avoid the same mistakes and reroute around the relationship pitfalls.

HE ASKED

1. Do you think that keeping a score with your partner is a productive way of managing equal effort?

2. If you find yourself keeping score, is it time to reassess to see if you are playing by the rules?

3. Are you willing to give up your shot at the title to become a part of the team?

Chapter 11: Perfection in Imperfection

SHE SAID

Andy's mom said to me very early on in my relationship with her son, "If you ever figure him out, would you let me know?" I thought it a bit of an odd question since she'd known him for almost fifty years, but it does speak to the fact that he's not your typical man. He's one in a million, my Andy, but he does lack most normal human emotions. I don't play poker, and I don't think he does either, but the man's facial expressions hardly ever change. I never know if he's telling the truth, lying, or joking. He's a puzzle that constantly needs solving because the pieces seem to keep changing.

Andy isn't perfect, but neither am I. He has serious ADHD, but I'm a control freak. Our wedding photographer had to tell me three times to "let him" dip me for that iconic picture pose . . . I have serious control issues. No one is perfect, but someone can be perfect for you; your flaws simply need to match up and fill in the spaces to form a complete piece. Andy is completely lacking any organizational skills, but my organization skillset makes up for it. I make a weekly dinner menu simultaneously with the shopping list and a weather forecast, and then I rewrite the list based on the store layout to maximize efficiency. I'm the world's worst listener, but he remembers everything I say. His time management skills are nonexistent, but I think ten steps down the line. I'm great with technology, and he says that when he retires, he doesn't even want to deal with an email address. I'm a total spaz, and he's always calm and collected. I get lost in the details, and he brushes little things off.

He and I couldn't be more opposite, and on paper, we don't make any sense. I'm a straight-A student who never needed a curfew, never smoked a cigarette, never got grounded, never got drunk, and has always followed the rules. He's the serial dater douche canoe who went to raves, got covered in tattoos, loved to start bar fights, and was a stripper. What can I say? Opposites do attract. It's a bit shocking how little we have in common, but we work so great together; it's weird and wonderful. So many people have told me that at first glance, he's not who they would have pictured I'd be with, but he gives me grace in my weak areas because he knows he's strong in that area, and vice versa. We are both so strong in our strengths and so weak in our weaknesses that we are imperfectly perfect for each other.

I admit that I struggle a little more than he does when granting grace. I mean, I can't explain to you how horrible of a listener I am, and when he's trying to tell me something, in the few moments he speaks, I usually hear him pause to ask, "You're not listening, are you?" Again, an area I'm trying to suck less at. When the absentminded husband does something well within the realm of Andrew's absentmindedness, I nitpick, but I'm working on it because he's worth it.

The best way to illustrate our perfection in imperfection is the story of the wedding ring debacle. Andy and I picked out my engagement ring together, and at the time, I said I didn't need or want a wedding band. Well, that was stupid. Andy, of course, knew I'd change my mind. I went back to the store and purchased the wedding band after I decided I needed it. After the wedding, however, I went into a local jewelry store to see about having the two rings soldered together, and the salesperson asked which side of the pear-shaped engagement diamond I wanted the wedding band mounted to. If I had known the bands were made ambidextrously, I would have purchased two when they were on sale!

What did I do when I was driving home from the jewelry store? I called Andy and told him that for Christmas, I needed another wedding band, and then I would get all three soldered. "Needed" is the key word. Good husband that he is, Andy came through on Christmas morning with a second wedding band. But wait, why wasn't it aligning perfectly with the arches on the engagement band?

"Did you order the one I sent you the link to?" I asked hesitantly, trying to hide my disappointment and not seem like an ungrateful witch.

"Yes, why?" he cautiously responded.

"Well, it doesn't fit as well as the other one does," I explained.

"Well, that figures. I always screw things up," he muttered.

After wearing the unattached, mismatched set for a little while, I decided to keep that second band, flaws and all. While I'm a total perfectionist, I looked at the tiny mismatch as the perfect visual reminder of how our love is perfect in its imperfections. The ring that will live forever on my finger will be a constant reminder that while he may have little flaws, he's the perfect fit for me. I find myself looking at it often, and while it doesn't match up perfectly, it's one-in-a-million unique, and I smile knowing how hard he tried to make me happy . . . how hard he is always trying.

> *Dick was outside mowing and doing yard maintenance for hours. It was understood that he would handle those chores, and he was just fine with it. After he'd done a spectacular job of making the yard look groomed, he went upstairs to take a shower. Jane came home from running errands to see a trail of dirt and leaves from the back door to the stairs. Immediately enraged, she grabbed the vacuum, sucked up the mess, and berated Dick as soon as he appeared after his shower.*
>
> *All Dick had wanted from Jane was a little praise for the job he had done outside, but all Jane focused on was the particulates of dirt that he left on the floor. "Do you know how many times I vacuum after I come in from doing yard work?" he asked.*

"No, I didn't know that you did that," she admitted. She was sucking, and she started to feel bad. All of those hours that he worked in the yard and all of those times he vacuumed up his mess were unacknowledged and unappreciated, and all she did was focus on the one mistake.

"I'm sorry, honey," Jane said as her tone softened toward her husband. "I appreciate all of the things you do here, and the yard looks amazing."

"It's okay, Jane. Thank you for apologizing. I'll try to make sure I don't leave messes when I come in from doing yard work."

At first, Jane wasn't seeing the bigger picture and was sucking quite a bit at understanding Dick. The important thing is that she realized where she needed to improve and immediately made a correction for the sake of her marriage. Understanding yourself and your partner is paramount to finding your happiness in someone else's flaws. A few years into my relationship, I did figure out my Andy. Understanding his two core values helped me to be able to forgive and forget his imperfections more easily.

1. He loves me.
2. He would never intentionally do anything to hurt me.

How can these two short statements be all I need to know? Let's say he puts the ice cream scooper away in the wrong place. I know that he isn't doing it because he wants to irritate me or play some dumb mind game like, "If I do it wrong, she'll ask me to stop doing it." He is just legit absentminded but is doing his best to help me out by doing the dishes. It's all about controlling your snap reactions, pausing, and reminding yourself who your person is at his core.

If you always let your reactions guide your relationship, one or both of you will be unhappy. Plus, it's immature not to keep learning from your mistakes and not learning to control your emotions. If I get mad at him for putting the ice cream scooper away in the wrong place, and he thinks he's doing a good thing by doing and putting away the dishes, that mismatch of emotions and expectations will explode in your face. It's very demotivating when someone thinks they're doing something good for the other and still gets in trouble. That's when you'll hear guys say, "Nothing I ever do is right," and they start giving up.

I know it's hard, I know it's counterintuitive, and I know it will take time and effort to change your habits and your thinking, but if you want your relationship to be successful, you need to try. Think hard about your partner and his core relationship values. If his values are as simple and powerful as Andy's, then maybe you need to check yourself and change how you react. Men aren't always the bad guys in relationships; sometimes, it's our overthinking perception. Everyone can suck at any point, but the important thing to do is to realize that you suck and work toward sucking less.

Finding perfection in the imperfections is about forgiving and forgetting. It's about finding your counterpart in strengths and weaknesses and not punishing each other for their flaws. Instead, embrace their strengths and forgive their weaknesses, especially if they quickly forgive yours.

HE SAID

She: What do you think are your strengths and weaknesses as they pertain to relationships?

He: Patience is my biggest strength. I guess, uh (*pauses to take a big, loud inhale through his nose*) willingness . . .

She: (*Whispering*) A good listener . . .

He: Patience, good listener, and willingness to adapt. I'm not strongly opinionated about many things.

She: What are your weaknesses?

He: Obviously my lapses of memory, my absentmindedness, and my lack of attention to detail.

She: What do you think are my strengths and weaknesses in a relationship?

He: Inflexibility would be a weakness. Your drive is a benefit. Persistence, like, "I'm going to make this work regardless of what happens."

She: Determination.

He: Yeah, that's right. Determination. I don't know. I don't see very many weaknesses in you; I just don't see them. You're fairly inflexible, but you're also flexible because you adjust to handle the things I need, even though they would normally upset you. You overlook them because you see I'm not doing something wrong on purpose. That takes a certain amount of compassion and understanding, but you are NOT a good listener.

She: (*Laughing*) Yeah, I know.

He: You don't take people's feelings into account.

She: What?!

He: You just do what you want to do. (*Smiles*) And I'm okay with that.

She: What are you talking about!?

He: Like, "Oh, we're going to do this, and that's the way it is" and you just don't care. That's kind of how you are.

She: Oh, Mr. I-Don't-See-Many-Weaknesses-in-You, you want to pick THAT fight with me?

He: Well, that's just one. It's not a big deal, but in a relationship, it could be a big problem.

She: IS it a problem?

He: No, I'm just saying it could be. If you were in a relationship with someone who wasn't like me, it could probably cause a problem if there were two strong personalities.

She: Okaaaay. Well, why do you so easily forgive or overlook my weaknesses, like when I get short with you when we're trying to leave on time or when I suck at listening?

He: Because it doesn't bother me, and I don't take it personally. In those circumstances, I think, "It is what it is; I just have to endure it." That mindset might be part of my military training: "This sucks, but it'll only suck for a little bit of time, and you just get through it—don't take it personally, and . . ."

She: Embrace the suck?

He: Embrace the suck and drive on.

She: (*Laughing*) I feel like I've heard you say more than once, "I screwed up again. Typical." Why do you say that, and what do you hope to achieve by saying it?

He: I say it because it keeps me from blowing a gasket. It's not the end of the world; it's just something I do, and I can adapt to it because I've done it my whole life. I tell myself I'll adapt, overcome, succeed, and be okay. It can happen a thousand times a day, and I'll still survive.

She: So, it's essentially you reassuring yourself that it's okay to be flawed?

He: Well, I think that when you have a history of people telling you that you're messed up, it's okay to tell yourself that you're not. It's okay to be yourself, and it's okay that you do things the wrong way because you're only human, and it doesn't make you a bad person. It doesn't make you uncaring or unloving. It just means you're flawed, and you're learning to live with it. I do it to tell myself, "It happens; it's who you are . . ."

She: (*Giggling*) So, when you're doing the dishes, and I point out to you that you put something away in the wrong place, how does that make you feel? Are you less motivated to do the dishes the next time?

He: It doesn't make me feel anything (*Starts laughing*).

She: Okay, well, are you less motivated to do the dishes the next time?

He: No. I just look at it like, "Well, at least I tried putting them away."

She: What advice would you give couples to accept and move past someone's relationship weaknesses?

He: Move past them?

She: How do you deal with them and still have a successful relationship?

He: I've told this to my daughter at least sixteen times in the last frickin' year. You can see how a person is, and if you can accept that and say, "You know what, I still want to be with you even though you do x," then you must let it go. You have to decide right then and there that you're not going to bring it up, you're not going to harp on it, and you're not going to hold it against them. You're going to let it go, you're going to accept it, and you're going to love them for it.

If you can do that, then you're with the right person. If you can't do that because you can't change the person, that's when the problems start.

She: So, for better or worse.

He: Yes. There is no amount of yelling at your partner that will change their personality and who they are at their core. If that's your game, you'll always be unhappy, and you'll make the other person unhappy. Unfortunately, that's a mistake that many people make time and time again. If there's even just one thing you can't get over, it will come up again and again and again, and you'll use it in every argument, and it's going to destroy the relationship.

The simple fact is that no one (not me, not Jane, not you, and not Dick) is perfect. When it comes to working with someone else's weaknesses, you need to come up with systems to compensate for your strengths. If you can't forgive their little mistakes, you're not with the right person, or you're not emotionally healthy enough to be in a relationship. If you want someone to be able to forgive your weaknesses, then you should be willing to reciprocate if you love them. Mutual grace combined with mutual amounts of love will help you to find your own perfection in imperfection.

HE ASKED

1. What areas do you know your partner is weak in that you compensate for with your strengths?

2. What areas are you weak in that your partner makes up for with his strengths?

3. Do you find that one party seems more forgiving of the other's weakness?

Chapter 12: Communicate, Communicate, and Communicate Some More

SHE SAID

Have you ever watched a rom-com and been so frustrated and irritated that the couple isn't communicating in a way that would have easily solved the problem? You know I love a good rom-com, but I hear myself yelling at the TV like men yell at sports games: "If you just had a conversation, you wouldn't be running away in different directions when you're clearly meant for each other!" Duh. For as predictable, stupid, and repetitive as every one of these movies is, I can't help myself. I just can't.

When you watch a sport or a relationship from the outside, it's easy to see what the problems and solutions are. Why? Because you're not emotionally invested. Your pride, your dignity, your reputation, your friends and family, and your children aren't involved. When you're looking from a distance, the solution is simple: better communication. That "simple" solution becomes so much more complicated when it pertains to our own lives. Most of us suck at effective communication in our personal lives.

Take my husband, for example. He can deal with all sorts of craziness and drama when it happens while at work for the police department, but if there is even a glimmer of drama or craziness in his personal life, he can't deal with it, so he avoids it. There should be a decoder ring for relationship issues. You could look through a colored gem at your problems, and the issue and solution would be magically revealed.

The fact of the matter is everything is easier said than done when it comes to matters of the heart. Have you ever been in a restaurant seated near a couple that doesn't say one word to each other the whole time? Awkward. Did they run out of things to talk about, or have they simultaneously been struck mute? Are they so disinterested in what the other has to say or what happened to them that day that they'd rather sit in uncomfortable silence, in discomfort so thick that people around them can feel it?

The real problem with poor communication is that it can grow quickly and out of control if left unattended . . . like an untreated infection. When people leave things unsaid because they're too tired or feel disconnected from their partner, the space between them grows larger and larger. It's in the void of unspoken words that the festering spreads, infecting and seeping into other areas.

Why do we stop talking to our partners? There was a time when we stayed up until midnight talking because there was so much to say. How can you go from that to nothing? Are we embarrassed to ask for what we want? Are we afraid to hurt someone's feelings by telling them the truth? Are we just so tired of asking for the same thing over and over and getting nowhere that we give up?

Do we think, "What's the point?" It can be all these things. Life gets busy, life gets complicated, and life changes. If you aren't communicating effectively with your partner through these changes, you may never find the cure for the silent infection.

Communication in a relationship includes talking about what you need and expect from your partner, what has changed and why it has changed, and how unwanted changes can be fixed. If you constantly complain to your bestie about the same issues with your partner, that probably means you should be talking through those issues with your partner, not slandering their character behind their back. It's the same concept as complaining about your job or your workplace to your work spouse. At work, if you have issues that you cannot move past, you communicate those issues in a meeting with your supervisor. Change doesn't happen by wishing it or willing it; you need to make it happen, but making it happen is hard and uncomfortable, which is why so many people shy away from it.

> *Jane has asked Dick an innumerable number of times to put his shoes out of the way when he comes home. She cannot even count how many times she has tripped over them or had the back door not open all the way because it got hung up on his shoes. She had gotten so frustrated that every time she tripped on his shoes, she reacted by yelling, "Seriously, Dick! Are you kidding me? I don't know how many times I have asked you to put your shoes out of the way so I don't trip on them. I don't know why you don't get it!"*

Silence. "Did you hear me?!" she berated. After each blowout, things continued as they had before. No change. Jane found herself wondering if Dick needed to go to the doctor to have his hearing tested. Was he even listening to her anymore? She was stuck and didn't know what else she could do to get him to hear her and do what she asked.

Jane's problem wasn't the message she was trying to convey to Dick. There's nothing wrong with wanting your husband to be more conscious of where he put his shoes. The issue was with how she communicated with him—or at him, rather.

In relationships, if you want to communicate effectively, you need to consider your approach. If you "communicate" by yelling at your partner when you're in the thick of something that's bothering you, that's not good communication. That's you yelling, and no one ever hears anything or is receptive to anything when they're being attacked. I know that as an adult if someone yells at me, I'm not inclined to change. I'm inclined to do the opposite of what they want.

When I feel ready to freak out at Andy, I take a deep, slow breath in and out before I say anything. That short pause can diffuse 100 percent psycho to at least 45 percent crabby before I speak. If you have a long list of grievances with your partner, you need to schedule a time to have a conversation: no interruptions, no kids, no phones, no TV on in the background, and no distractions. Both parties can come to the table with their grievances and have a calm conversation. If you handle conflict resolution like a work meeting and separate the conversation from the explosive in-the-moment emotions, you're in a better place to have a productive discussion.

I learned this communication technique when I hosted foreign Au Pairs. With my first Au Pair from Germany, I immediately got after her when I had an issue with something she was doing. Communicating in the moment often brings strong emotions, and one party feels attacked. The second Au Pair agency that we used to find our second Au Pair from Ukraine asked me to help other potential host families talk through would-be issues. In those conversations, I always advocated for the weekly meetings at the beginning. While everything was so new for both parties, the meetings needed to take place when the children were asleep, and both parties could come to the table knowing it was a safe place to discuss any issues.

> *Jane approached Dick and confessed that something wasn't working and she wasn't feeling heard. She suggested that instead of date night, they would keep the sitter but would take that time and meet to discuss marital business. She asked Dick to come up with a list of things that he thought they needed to work on, and she said she would do the same. During their meeting, she had a much easier time logically speaking to Dick, "Dick, I would really appreciate if you would put your shoes out of the way when you come home. I know you're tired, but sometimes I trip on them, and it would mean a lot*

to me if you could try to remember to put them to the side of the entry."

"I'm sorry. I didn't understand why my shoes were making you so upset. I thought maybe you were mad at me for something else. I'll try to do better," Dick responded.

Dick expressed to Jane that he doesn't like to get nagged, and he would appreciate some leeway with the things she asks him to do. "If you tell me when you need something done by, I'll try to get it done, but I can't always drop everything to do something right when you ask," he explained. Because they handled the conversation with respect and a calm and receptive attitude, they both felt heard and left the discussion holding hands.

When you communicate with your spouse, respect is a must-have. Without it, your communication will never be effective. People get way too comfortable with their significant others, and they forget pleasantries that they would never overlook when speaking with others. They forget how to be nice to their partners. In your spousal meetings, try to speak in "I" statements like, "When you do this, I feel like that." Not, "I hate it when you do this!" See the difference? Someone can't argue with how something makes you feel, but they'll get defensive if they feel attacked. What do you think an animal would do if it felt threatened? It wouldn't listen calmly and then behave. We, like animals, will act instinctually. After all, we are only animals with thumbs, bigger brains, and sometimes nice manicured nails.

Before and during your predetermined relationship meeting, try to find a way to remind yourself to stay calm. However, if things are escalating, someone is yelling, or respect is thrown out the window, then you need to take a break and reschedule. If it gets so bad that neither party is feeling heard or one party is feeling attacked, then it's time to bring in the professionals. A mediator can hold a mirror up to your behavior. People always tone down their emotions toward their partners when there's someone else in the room. They're on their best behavior, and that's why people seek professional help.

I have offered to be that third party for some of my friends, but no one has taken me up on it. I'm only trying to help them suck less! If you take a moment to look at why you explode at your partner, most of the time, you're attacking your partner so aggressively, which has nothing to do with anything they did. You're simply on edge and are taking it out on them because you're stressed at work, or you didn't get enough sleep, or you're hungry. You're taking it out on them because they are your safe place. They are your home where you can let it all out and be yourself because you know that love and forgiveness reside there. It's like how your child could be perfectly respectful and a good listener in school, but they're sassy and rude to you at home. They are this way because they feel safe knowing that if they freak out at you, they know you'll love them anyway. Many parents who have attended parent-teacher conferences know what I'm talking about.

Great communication is certainly not one of the easiest things to check off your relationship goals checklist because it's not a one-and-done achievement. You almost need a chart like an employee of the week chart. For every week of successful communication (meaning that both parties are happy at the end of the week), you can put a gold star on the chart WITHOUT arguing about who gets to place the gold star.

Think before you speak when communicating with your partner, be respectful, set up a meeting to air any grievances, and store your issues safely on a list that is reserved for the meeting. You'll be surprised to look back at your list and realize some of those things that were so important at the moment aren't an issue anymore because the issue was your own triggers. If you, both of you, can establish some communication best practices and retrain your brains, you can keep putting those gold stars on your relationship goals chart together.

HE SAID

She: Have you been in relationships where you know poor communication was the reason they ended?

He: Yeah, every one of them ended because of poor communication.

She: Okay, it sounds like you're not trying.

He: That's how I feel about it.

She: You don't want to try?

He: I'm saying that's the reason all relationships end.

She: (*Sarcastically*) Is it though???

He: People haven't found a way to communicate their needs to the other person, and . . .

She: Sometimes the other person can't give you that.

He: Well, that's the thing you should figure out. Relationships can end from either good or bad communication. If you have good communication and can find out early that you're not the right fit for each other, it ends. If you have bad communication and realize you can't communicate, it ends.

She: Why do you think that it's so hard for couples to maintain effective communication?

He: Because life is hard.

She: PSHTTTH!

He: Good communication stands strong in bad times or in good. That's the key. If you value and love your partner, and if they do the same, you'll find a way to make it work. People get together for one reason or another, but then, when something changes over time, people need to be able to communicate unhappiness with the change in a supportive way.

Can you communicate what you need before it's too late for them to return to who they were before?

She: Hmmm. Okay. What are some things that you think couples should communicate more about? Like certain topics that you think are hard for people to talk about.

He: Am I still the person you fell in love with? Is there something I could do better to get back to that person? Am I still attractive to you?

She: I think that the letting-yourself-go conversation is hard when you think the other person isn't pulling their weight in that department. No pun intended.

He: Well, you need to be willing to take whatever they say. If I come to you and say, "Are you still attracted to me anymore? I want you to be honest, and I'm not going to be mad if you aren't still attracted to me." If you respond with, "No, I'm not because of this and this and this," then I have to be a man of my word and not get upset or offended by it; I'm going to try to make it better.

She: Okay, but that's you asking for advice about you. What about someone . . .

He: No, I'm saying that I've got to trust my partner, think of a way that I can say something to her about my desires, and not worry about her being upset with me.

She: You don't think a woman would be upset if you said she needed to lose a couple of pounds?

He: Yeah, but if it's that important to you, you gotta say something about it, otherwise you won't be happy.

She: Do you think WE have good, effective communication in our relationship, and why?

He: I think we do, but I think it can always get better.

She: Who's sucking more?

He: I don't think either one of us is. I think we both have the ability to be comfortable enough to say things to each other and not worry about it being taken the wrong way. You can say pretty much anything to me, and you don't have to worry about me freaking out because I've shown in my behavior that's not how I'll react to things.

She: Like when I tell you in the winter that you're getting fat?

He: Yeah, but there needs to be consistency in behavior and reactions for someone to feel comfortable in that delicate subject.

She: So, if someone always overreacts to everything, you're not going to come to them with, "Well, maybe you need to work on . . . whatever."

He: It's also important what partner you choose at the beginning of your relationship. You need to pick someone that's mature enough to be able to take constructive criticism. For me, I would never be with somebody who didn't take care of themselves physically and didn't look attractive to me. I just wouldn't do it, so I've always made it clear at the beginning of relationships.

She: Yeah, but no. What about women who think, "He's going to love me regardless of having kids . . ."

He: No, no, no. Absolutely not.

She: (*Laughing*)

He: Absolutely not true. (*Not laughing*) He may still love you, but he won't be attracted to you. You can love someone but not be in love with them or want to be with them.

She: We're going off-topic. What do you think are the keys to good communication in a relationship?

He: Well, intimacy is in there. Intimacy's a big deal, and trust.

She: In communication?

He: Yeah. There needs to be a lot of intimacy and trust in communication.

She: Emotional intimacy, not physical intimacy, yes?

He: Yeah. Trust, intimacy, compassion, and respect are all important to communication because people yell at each other, and that's not respectful. If you scream at someone at the top of your lungs and you flip out, your partner won't feel safe talking to you. You also need to be open to hearing things you might not want to hear, and you need to take ownership of the fact that you're not perfect and don't take what your partner says as a personal attack.

You just need to be a reasonable person, and you have to express the things that you want for yourself.

There are so many ways in which we communicate with the world and with our partners. There's body language, talking, passive-aggressive social media posts, yelling, giving the silent treatment, and so many more. I always shake my head when someone tries to use social media to communicate with her partner. Passive aggressive memes aimed at your partner in hopes that he will be able to read your mind are pretty childish. You're making a lot of assumptions with that methodology, and it will never work. If that's you, stop it. Stop it right now.

Relying on social media posts to fix your relationship is the pinnacle of idiocy. "Happy anniversary to my husband. Here's to another twenty years of happiness." That man better be the first to like and comment on her post if he wants to keep in her good graces. Someone, please remind me how old we are again. Andy doesn't have social media, but I do. I think it helps our relationship that one of us doesn't because there are no expectations or attempts at using it as a legitimate form of communication.

Good communication in a relationship needs to apply not only to verbal but also non-verbal interactions with each other. I've seen some glares that could slice a person in half, and everyone has experienced or given the silent treatment at least once. If you approach your scheduled relationship meetings, the ones I encouraged you to make to discuss grievances, with your arms crossed and a scowl on your face, you've already failed. Graduating to the next level in communication will require the highest grades in Maturity 201 and Respect 304. Figure out a way to control your childish reactions and learn how to speak to your partner with respect like you would speak to a coworker in a professional setting. If you yell at a co-worker, you face the risk of losing your job. If you yell at your partner, you face the risk of losing your relationship.

If you can get those straight A's and make permanent changes to how you communicate, you may even be able to graduate with honors into the elite society of successful long-term relationships.

HE ASKED

1. Do you value peace in your relationship more than you value always winning every argument?

2. Are you willing to recognize when your emotions take over in an argument, and are you willing to come up with a process to diffuse your anger before you approach your partner?

3. Are you open to creating a safe environment for both parties to be able to share any issue, no matter how difficult it may be to talk about?

Chapter 13: Your Partner Should NOT Be Your Best Friend

SHE SAID

"Today, I will marry my best friend." It's the phrase almost every couple says at their wedding. I'm sorry, but . . . lame! I always roll my eyes when someone says their partner is their best friend. It's not that I don't believe in love; I'm a huge cheerleader for love, but a bestie and a life partner are not interchangeable.

When Andy and I got engaged and discussed our very small wedding guest list, I asked him who his best friend was. Stupidly, I assumed he'd say it was me, but he never says what I think he will say. After I got over the hurt of not being chosen as his best friend, I remembered that it's healthy for relationships when each party has besties outside of the relationship.

Stop making that disgusted face; let me explain. I'm not saying that your partner shouldn't be the person you share everything with, the person you call first when there's any news to share, or the person you look to for comfort when something bad happens. They totally should be. But isn't that the very definition of a best friend? Not really. Your spouse's job in your relationship is to be your life partner, not your best friend. My best friend was the one fluffing my dress at our intimate backyard wedding, and Andy's best friend was the guy who did everything possible to be there even though he was extremely ill.

Your best friend is the person you go to when you want to talk about your partner, the second phone call you make, and the person who gets you because they're likely the same gender . . . likely. Why am I okay with my husband not being my best friend and vice versa? You don't want to fall into the trap of putting too much pressure on your mate. Being a life partner is pressure enough, but asking them to be your best friend, your therapist, your fixer, your shoulder to cry on, your shopping partner, your dining partner, your activity partner, your co-host at dinner parties, and your party or concert plus one is too much. Assuming that your partner's tastes and hobbies will be exactly the same as yours is pretty naïve.

It's healthy to have a life outside of your relationship. Separating the role of bestie and partner gives your partner room to breathe. My husband is an extreme introvert, so I plan parties and dinners with my friends when he's not at my house. He thanks me for it, for getting my extrovertedness out in the company of other people. I know him well enough to know that he would rather I chit-chat about all things meaningless with a friend for hours than bore him on the phone while he interjects the occasional "uh huh" or "yeah." When I have some news and am looking for an equally matched level of excitement, I call my bestie. When I call Andy, I get zero emotion and never get what I think I should get, but I know that and understand that he's a robot.

Here's a classic example of expectation versus reality. Andy and I have planned a trip for early next year to a five-star, all-inclusive resort in the Bahamas for my forty-third birthday. Our airfare was rebooked by the airline and needed to be fixed so our travel agent could negotiate a room upgrade for our stay. We went from mid-level luxury to a butler elite honeymoon suite with a Rolls Royce transfer from the airport. "I'm so excited! I can't wait to tell Andy!" I told the travel agent. I couldn't reach him for some reason, so I called my bestie. We screamed with equally matched, high-pitched shrieks of excitement—the normal response most people would have. The response most women would experience with their best friends.

When my husband finally called me back, what did he say?

"I would rather have had them give us a discount on the room we already booked," he said in his typical monotone cadence.

"Seriously?" I was annoyed that he didn't share my excitement.

I mean, the man tells me to get a boyfriend when he's not at my house, so he doesn't have to deal with my complaints about things breaking when I'm alone. He's not serious, I don't think.

Andy calls me on his way home to his house from work, but if my best friend calls a few minutes into the conversation, he will gladly hand me over to someone who enjoys talking because it gets him off the hook. I realize that not every man is as extreme as my husband when it comes to conversation aversion, but men and women communicate and relate differently, and it's so helpful to have someone else to talk to other than your mate. Furthermore, if you talk too much at your mate, they stop listening. Yes, at, not with. I'm convinced that if you engage in talking at your partner too much, the little sound receptor hairs in his ear depress permanently, making him truly deaf to the sound of your voice.

I knew this lady once who had a dating team: one guy to go to the movies with, one guy to go to restaurants with, one guy for sex, one guy for nights in, and one guy for conversation. Extreme as her team approach to dating was, it kind of makes sense in reference to taking the burden off your partner. I have friends whom I like to do specific things with:

1. one who likes driving (I hate driving), so we drive north and hike
2. ones whom I have play dates with (whose children play well with my children)
3. ones whom I go to dinner with
4. ones whom I talk reality dating shows with
5. ones I can do weekday lunches with
6. ones whom I only see at my parties because their lives are crazy busy.

Having a diverse group of friends and family helps take all the pressure off your partner, allowing your relationship the breathing room it needs to grow and not be suffocated. A healthy relationship needs an outside network rich in different interests and strengths to be successful. When you spend some time away from your spouse doing something you enjoy with someone else who shares that same interest, your partner then has an opportunity to do the same or do nothing if he so chooses. Time away from your partner is an absolute necessity for a healthy relationship. Without time apart, how can you ever miss them or have something exciting to talk about?

If you're an introvert, spending time away from your partner doing something you like could just mean going it alone. If you like hiking in nature, but he wants to watch football, go take a hike. Literally. If you want to see a movie you know he won't like, go by yourself. You won't have to share the popcorn. Introverts can feel comfortable alone, but they still need to find interests outside of their relationship. The same rule of separation applies, but it has fewer players.

When two people spend too much time together, they start to get annoyed with every little thing their partner does. My parents owned a small-town grocery store/gas station together for twenty-one years. Their pact was that whoever asked for a divorce would have to take the business. They knew that they spent too much time together and that it would make their marriage more difficult to sustain over time. The pact, odd as it was, acknowledged the issue of too much time together and offered a solution of sorts. Well, a threat, I guess. Similarly, my ex-husband and I both worked from home and sometimes a house can't be big enough.

> *When Jane met Dick, she had just moved to a new town and didn't have family or friends nearby. Jane was so lucky to have met someone that she could spend her free time with. However, she found herself relying on him for something almost every day of the week: entertainment, company, or conversation. If Dick was busy, she didn't know what to do with herself. If he didn't text her back, she ruminated about why he was ignoring her. She became obsessed. Dick had become her whole world, and the relationship started to fall apart. Dick felt smothered and thought she was needy, and Jane felt like he didn't care about her enough to give her everything she was asking of him. He started pulling away, and she didn't understand what was happening.*
>
> *Jane turned to her best friend, "What is happening? I don't understand why he's pulling away," she whined.*
>
> *"Maybe you need to find a hobby to take some of the pressure off of Dick," her bestie suggested.*
>
> *"I guess so, but I don't know what that would be," Jane confessed. "I think you're right, though; maybe I can volunteer at the shelter."*
>
> *"That's a great idea! Then when you do see Dick, you'll have more to talk about, and maybe you'll make new friends there too," her bestie advised.*

Signing up to volunteer was the best thing Jane did for her relationship with Dick. He got some room to breathe, she expanded her friend circle, and the separation and space helped them grow closer together. Eventually, they got married.

When you put a little distance between you and your partner by doing things you enjoy with other people with similar interests, the more you'll think positively about your partner. Sometimes, you'll even miss their flaws . . . but you need to spend days apart for that little miracle. I'm certainly not suggesting that you don't allocate any quality free time with your partner; it is very important to introduce your significant other to your interests and hobbies, and vice versa. However, if they've tried and tried to like what you like, but you know they're miserable, love them for trying, and activate your friends and family or solo hobbyist plan.

When I worked in long-term senior care, I could see how very differently men and women handled being left alone due to the death of a spouse. Men tended to put more stock in their wives as their only best friends, and women typically had friends along with having a partner. When a man loses his wife, he loses his cook, maid, planner, activity director, confidant, and comfortable place. Typically, wives are the ones who make the social plans. So, when she's gone, he is lost and alone.

Women, however, when they lose a husband, rely on their friends to help them through. While it is a sad situation to witness, I saw more lonely single men in assisted living than I did any lonely single women. Women went to activities, gathered in each other's rooms to share a drink, found commonalities, had after-hours ice cream parties, and made new friends. I tried to start men's group activities, but getting men to emerge from their lonely but comfortable caves was quite challenging. Granted, these seniors were of a different generation with slightly different values, but their situations highlight the importance of friends and relationships outside of marriage.

When you arrive at your golden years, you realize that people matter most, more than things or accomplishments. Things and accomplishments can't do a lot for your mental state when you're stuck in assisted living. Those seniors cherish visits from friends and family more than gold.

In leaving my job as the Life Enrichment Director at a senior living facility, I wanted to take some of my friends with me. Taking all of them wasn't an option, but not taking any was also not an option. I thought carefully about who I could adopt as a grandparent into my personal life, and my friend Nancy was the one. She had lost most of her family, her daughters, her husband, and some grandchildren, and I had no more grandparents left. I truly enjoy her company, dirty sense of humor, and creativity, and she was one of the few non-family guests at my wedding. We get together about once a month, and being with her reminds me how important human connections and family are.

What I'm trying to emphasize is that you need to expand your network beyond your partner. Both of you should. Don't guilt him about his poker nights or fantasy football leagues. Encourage them. Hire a babysitter and multitask by using those times to go to dinner or go out shopping with your friends. When you come back together at the end of the day for quality time or a date night, you'll have interesting things to talk about, things that light you up and breathe energy back into your relationship.

HE SAID

She: Am I your best friend?

He: Hmmm. That's kind of a hard . . .

She: (*Smugly*) There's no punishment; we have safe communication, remember?

He: I'm trying to think of what a smart answer would be.

She: (*Laughing*) There's only one of two answers.

He: You have to say it with some kind of justification.

She: I will ask follow-up questions; just answer the question.

He: (*Long pause.*)

She: Am. I. Your. Best. Friend? If not, who is?

He: (*Still thinking*) Yeah, I guess you are.

She: Dammit! Well, do you think it's normal or healthy for someone's spouse NOT to be their best friend?

He: Yeah.

She: Why?

He: I think you should have someone you can communicate to about things you won't share with your significant other. You must have that outlet; I think that's a huge thing.

She: Have you been in a relationship where your partner told you that you WERE her best friend?

He: No.

She: No?

He: No.

She: Huh.

He: I think that it was always known they wouldn't be my best friend, but I think it's different when you're married.

She: Is it?

He: You spend so much more time together with that person than you do with other people.

She: Do you think couples should do everything together?

He: No.

She: What goes through your mind when I ask you to watch a reality dating show or go shopping?

He: I don't mind shopping, but I hate reality shows.

She: (*Snickers*) Do you ever think, "I wish she had a friend that she would do this with?"

He: No, I just wish I didn't have to do it.

She: (*Laughing*)

He: I don't care who has to do it; I just wish it wasn't me.

She: Do you think it's important for couples to have their own best friends outside of the relationship?

He: As long as it's the same sex and not a different sex friend.

She: Okay . . . you didn't answer the way I thought you were going to.

He: What did you think I was going to say?

She: I don't know.

While, for some reason, Andy has changed his view on having a best friend outside of our marriage, I think the only reason he doesn't is that his friend doesn't live anywhere near either of his homes—his or mine. Maybe when he retires, he can resume a life of free time outside of spending it with me and my children, but our situation is complicated by distance. However, he has told me he doesn't want to make any new friends. I think he'll be the introvert doing solo hobbies when I'm at work . . . something like kayaking on Lake Superior or biking on the Superior Hiking Trail. Right now, his solo hobby is working out.

"Did you have a good workout? Did anything weird happen at the gym? Was your gym nemesis there?" I ask.

Although he sees me as his best friend at this moment in time, he does communicate regularly with others at work or via text. We spend enough time apart simply due to the long-distance component of our relationship, and in those days away, we accumulate things to talk about in our separate lives. Having friends and family to whom we allocate time shows the other person that we are well-rounded, non-needy, healthy partners with independent social lives and brains of our own. Smothering each other won't happen when you diversify your relationship portfolio.

If you don't have a bestie outside of your relationship, you can always give that slot to a close family member or a hobby. Everyone needs someone else to talk to occasionally; it's healthy, your partner will be grateful, and it will only make your relationship stronger and more interesting.

HE ASKED

1. If you had exciting news to share, and your partner wasn't available, who would be the next three people you would contact?

    a. If you struggled to come up with three names, you may need to work on expanding your network of friends beyond your significant other.

2. If you couldn't post anything related to your relationship on your social media, what three other things would you post about?

    a. If you cannot come up with three things, chances are, you may need to find some hobbies or interests that are not tied to being in a relationship.

3. If you did a side-by-side comparison of your "pre-relationship life" and your "in-a-relationship life," would your "in-a-relationship life" be the same as your "pre-relationship life" except with extra things added on?

Chapter 14: "He Won't Bring You Flowers Anymore," the Nasty Naysayers Say

SHE SAID

Have you ever met those people, you know, the ones who take someone's happiness and rain all over it with negativity? These people cannot find happiness in their own lives, so they cannot fathom it in someone else's. "You just wait until you live together and his crap is everywhere . . ." So, I'm to believe that as soon as my husband moves in to live with me full time that the foundation of our relationship will crumble, we will become petty and immature, our effective communication will break down, and our relationship will be doomed to die a painful death? I don't think so.

My dad, one of the bluntest, matter-of-fact people I know, would continually say to me in the early years of dating Andy, "He won't bring you flowers anymore after you're married." In my happy, fairytale la la land, I would be instantly deflated mid-story of how Andy had brought me flowers again for no reason. Why you gotta be like that, Dad? He's from a different generation of men, and he's my dad, so he gets a pass.

I'm not a silly, doe-eyed girl who's delusional about how relationships grow and change and encounters hurdles that need to be worked through. This marriage isn't my first rodeo, and I am fully aware that relationships are hard and require lots of effort from both parties. However, I do not believe having a successful, communicative relationship is unattainable, even though many relationships cannot find mutual happiness and fail.

Being a naysayer is something I'm totally guilty of too. When I found myself unhappy in my first marriage, I would scoff at couples who were blissfully entering into marriage and would roll my eyes at weddings. I was a negative naysayer before, and I wasn't happy, so of course, I didn't believe it was possible in a long-term relationship.

"Just wait until you've been married ten years, then you'll see!" I said, doling out my sage wisdom upon unsuspecting, happy fools in love.

There is no more perfect manifestation of misery's loving company than when it comes to relationships. Happy people want to talk to happy people, and miserable people want to commiserate with the like. When people who are happy and blissful in their relationships end up faced with someone miserable, then a storm breaks out.

Neither side of the happiness coin wants to listen to the other because the other person's reality is incomprehensible. People surround themselves with like-minded people. That's simply a fact of life.

Now that I've crossed over from the dark side, I try to bridge the gap and offer a helping hand to those stuck in the quagmire of a struggling relationship. "Here, take my hand, and I'll help you out of the hole and into the light where I am."

It's not an easy climb up and out of the pit of despair, but this is why I'm sharing my happy wisdom with you.

Back to the flowers, a commonly contested gesture that usually ends after the courting phase of a relationship. Bring up flowers regarding relationships with any woman, and there's a pretty good chance that you'll likely get a lengthy rant. Go ahead; try it.

Early on in my relationship with Andy, I let him know how much I love a bouquet of fresh flowers. Month after month, year after year, Andy has proven with time and consistency that he will buy me flowers regularly and for no reason, so why would I assume that anything would change? Just because it has happened to others in their relationships doesn't mean it is a certainty in mine, does it? Sigh. Why can't people be happy for happy people? We need more positivity and optimism in this world.

One year, on our annual pilgrimage to visit Andy's family in Iowa for Thanksgiving, his mom asked me if I wanted a large crystal vase that she had nowhere to display.

"Sure, I'll take it. Andy is always buying me flowers," I said cheerfully as I cradled the crystal like a fragile baby in my arm.

"Andy will keep it full," his mom replied with a knowing smile.

Ever since that vase moved into its new home years ago, it hardly ever sits on the sidelines, empty of blooms. When it brightens my kitchen with sparkle and unprompted for-no-reason flowers, I smile every day and remember how much he loves me. Andy is such a thoughtful husband. I remember one time when he brought home flowers that matched the color scheme I designed on my new Christmas tree. Now that's next level, A+ husband behavior. He got a ton of points for that gesture!

After he had established a pattern of flower buying, I asked Andy, "If it's so simple and easy, why don't more men buy flowers for no reason?"

"Buying flowers at least once a month is like investing fifteen dollars into your relationship. It's not that much money in the grand scheme of things," he explained, "but the investment grows in her positive feelings for you."

He's right. Think of how much money you spend monthly on coffee, gas station snacks, or video games. Fifteen dollars is not that much money, and your investment will continue to mature and grow beyond your expectations.

I am going out on a limb here, but I would think that most men wouldn't want flowers as much as a woman would, but sometimes, to create an environment of giving, you may need to be the one who starts it. Remember when the pay-it-forward movement happened? People would pay for the next person in line's coffee or food, and the thoughtfulness spread.

In her marriage, Jane started letting the negativity of others' failing relationships seep into her own. Her coworkers always seemed to have an issue with their partners, and she started to overanalyze her own marriage. "Why doesn't he bring me flowers anymore? He knows my favorite flowers are carnations. They're like the cheapest ones," she said as she hopped onto the partner-bashing water cooler conversation.

After ruminating about her marriage all day at work and getting absolutely no work accomplished, Jane called her friend, who pushed, "I don't want to be rude, but what do you do for him that shows him how much you love him? Why is it always up to the man to be the one constantly courting his wife?" Silence.

"Yeah, I guess. I hadn't really thought about it like that," she confessed.

The next day, Jane made a special stop at the grocery store and bought the ingredients to make Dick's favorite cake. She worked extra hard to make it before he came home, and he was happily surprised. He swept her up in a passionate hug, and he held her. "Thank you. I had a rough day at work, and you've made this day so much better," he told her.

A few days later, a small bouquet of carnations and a card arrived at Jane's office. The card read, "Just because. Love, Dick." She was happy, but she also realized that she shouldn't let what other people say affect the happiness she has in her own relationship.

If you feel like you need more little investments in your relationship, maybe you should be the one who starts it like Jane did. Find little ways to show your partner how much he means to you. Put a six-pack of his favorite beer in the refrigerator, make him his favorite dessert, and give him a back rub. If you start the trend and the love in your relationship is strong, your partner will do something thoughtful for you.

I'm going to sound like my dad, but if you invest early and keep investing regularly into your retirement account, you'll be able to retire comfortably. Thanks, Daaaaaaad. The flower investment is no different, and it doesn't even have to be flowers. It doesn't have to be something big, elaborate, or expensive, but it does have to be done without strings attached, without expectations of anything in return, and it must be done for no reason. Easy peasy.

When it comes to those little investments, sometimes all you need to do is pull your selfish head out of your rear and suck less. No scorecard says he has to start it first; you can do it too. Prove all of those negative naysayers wrong about your relationship.

Naysayers can say all they want, but if you're in a strong, healthy, loving relationship, there's nothing they can say that will negatively impact your success and happiness. Absolutely nothing.

HE SAID

She: Have you ever had someone rain on your relationship happiness with negative comments based on their lack of success?

He: No.

She: You haven't had someone outside your relationship say anything? Your mom? Or . . .

He: No. No.

She: Didn't your daughter always tell you that you were going to die alone?

He: Yeah, but that was something else.

She: Okay, you're not helping here.

He: I don't think those are good questions.

She: Have you ever been a relationship naysayer to someone else?

He: No.

She: You're sucking at this chapter!

He: I always tell people that you have to be true to yourself and make a decision so you don't hurt the other person's feelings.

She: Yeah, I know. Why do you think people can be so pessimistic about relationships with people who are happy?

He: Because people aren't happy with themselves, and they don't like to see other people happy. That's just the way it is. I don't like those kinds of people, people that are negative, and I won't have them in my life. They don't give good advice, and you don't want negativity from an outside source coming into your relationship. It's just bad.

Letting an outsider in who is trying to separate you is disrespectful to the relationship.

She: But what if it's your friend who just says stuff even if you don't take it to heart?

He: Still, it leaks in by just hearing it. If you allow negative energy to leak into you, it will find a crack.

She: So, you just have to cut those people off then?

He: Just be honest with them and say, "Listen, I appreciate your concern for me, but if you have a suggestion that would be beneficial, I'll listen to that, but I don't want to hear your negativity about my relationship." That's a relationship killer.

She: Do you think women do it more than men?

He: Oh, way more. Guys would never do that. Because a guy trusts another guy in knowing that he's going to do what's right, and we support each other. A guy will only give advice if someone asks for it; he won't just give unsolicited advice for no reason.

She: So, why do you think my dad kept saying that after we got married, you wouldn't buy me flowers anymore?

He: People say things like that because they don't do it, and they don't want to see someone else doing it because it would make them feel insignificant or inadequate. People don't like feeling that way.

She: Oh, well, that makes sense.

Not everyone is lucky enough to find their person, the one who loves unconditionally and forgives easily. Those unlucky people will be your little rainclouds—the ones that were not in the forecast and seem to pop up on a sunny day, downpour on you, get everything soaking wet, and then disappear suddenly. Yes, unfortunately, these naysayers may be friends or family that you value or are stuck with, but a truly successful and happy relationship cannot be brought down by little bits of doubt that are thrown at it. If, however, your relationship isn't solid as a rock, then some of those comments could start you down the path of doubt in your partner and your future.

Regardless, if you can spot these little rain clouds, you can bring your umbrella. These passing showers aren't tsunamis or category-five hurricanes. They may bring downpours, but they will be gone as soon as they arrive. Building a strong foundation based on effective communication, trust, and respect will keep the downpouring water out of the basement of your relationship, and the foundation won't crack.

If you have the strength of will and the fortitude, you may even try to help that raincloud turn into partial or full sun. Just as negativity can breed negativity, positivity can also be contagious

HE ASKED

1. Do you think your relationship is strong enough to ward off negative comments?

2. If your answer is "no," why do you think you are so easily persuaded to find flaws in your relationship?

3. Do you have enough positive energy in your relationship to outshine negativity from outside sources?

Chapter 15:
One Key to Rule Them All

SHE SAID

There is always one simple but oh-so-crucial piece of key advice I tell people when they ask about my relationship and why it's so successful: Start each day by asking yourself, "How can I make my partner's life better today?" It sounds so easy, but it's also very difficult to pull off consistently because most people are very selfish in relationships. "Why doesn't he ask me if I need help?" "He doesn't do anything nice for me anymore." It's all very me-centric. If you can approach your relationship with a focus on the happiness of the other person, and that person does the same, you simply cannot lose.

On a recent summer day, my husband and I planned to spend the day at our favorite beach. Being the organized one of the two of us, I pack everything for trips—day trips or overnight trips. In packing for the day at the beach, I thought about what snacks each of us might like to have. Andy doesn't usually eat lunch, but he likes snacks at the beach, so I packed him some grapes I had washed, plucked off the vines, and frozen for him. I also packed him some veggie chips and a single-serve smoothie that I make and freeze in small containers.

Around lunchtime at the beach, I asked him if he wanted a snack.

"What do you have?" he asked.

"I have frozen grapes, veggie chips, and a smoothie bomb for you," I answered.

He picked the grapes, which, by the way, are perfect on a hot summer day. As he was enjoying his frozen treat and relaxing on our beach blanket, I asked him what he was thinking about. Expecting the typical "nothing" answer, I was pleasantly surprised with his response.

"I was just thinking about how with all my past relationships, even at their high points, this one is two hundred percent better than any of them. Not one of them would have frozen grapes for me. It's not just the grapes, it's the experience . . . you play the music I like," he elaborated.

In the many bags of crap that I bring to the beach, there's a small portable speaker that I play the Steely Dan station on for him. Even though I don't particularly care for that music, I know how much he likes it because it reminds him of good times in his childhood. When we got home and emptied the back of all our sand-covered bags, I leaned sideways and looked past him to the empty hatchback and open tailgate.

"Are you going to shut the tailgate?" I asked with a hint of annoyance.

"I will, but I'm going to take the vacuum out and vacuum all of the sand out first."

I didn't see that coming. I always take the responsibility of de-sanding the car, washing the beach towels, emptying the cooler, and generally doing all of the post-beach day cleanups while also making supper. Why? Because I'm a control freak who sometimes struggles with taking her own advice about asking for help and not taking over.

His offering to take one of my self-appointed chores, even something so simple, meant a great deal to me, and I told him so. Every subsequent beach day we enjoyed that summer ended with his sand mitigation of my vehicle—even all the footwells! When I'm exhausted, crabby, and frustrated while making dinner after a day at the beach, he asks me how he can help. Now, that's priceless. I will take a husband who loves and cherishes me that much over a ten-carat diamond any day.

I know what you're thinking: How can I get MY partner to help voluntarily? To have someone offer to do things for you, you may need to start treating them as you would want to be treated, just like starting the pay-it-forward little love investments from the previous chapter that Jane learned. Yes, we learn that proverb early on in life, but in relationships, it can pay off with big rewards in so many ways. Unselfishness is unselfishness, and love is love. It doesn't matter who starts it, but it does matter who keeps it going.

One of the ways that I show love for others is by cooking or baking for them. When we first started dating, I baked all of Andy's favorite treats. Unfortunately for his waistline, he ended up asking me to stop because I was "making him fat." Not being able to show him that I loved him through food, I felt like I wasn't doing enough, so I started making and serving him breakfast every morning. When I make dinner, I make extra when possible so I can send leftovers home in single-serve containers to show him I love him even when he's at his house.

If you know the ways you show others you love them, then try to tap into one way you show your partner you love him and make his day better. Starting with one thing is not an insurmountable ask. Sometimes, the thing you do for each other is a daily chore. I cook, he does the dishes, and we both express gratitude to each other for our part. On other days, you'll see an opportunity to surprise the other with their favorite treat, coffee, or some words of affirmation.

Once you both start changing your mindset to putting the other person's happiness, comfort, and enjoyment before your own, your relationship will reach the extra credit level. Here are the important things to remember:

1. Never take for granted a daily chore that's done to help you.
2. Keep doing things for your partner despite your return on investment.

3. Always let your partner know how much you appreciate what they do for you. Always.

One of my personal goals in trying to make experiences great for my hubby is to do all I can, hoping to hear him say, "What a great, great day!" I love hearing this phrase because I want that feeling for him. He works hard, loves me so much, is such a good husband, and is a wonderful stepfather. All I want is for him to be happy.

There's a bonus to this kind of selfless behavior if you have children. If they see you expressing gratitude and helping each other, they'll start doing it too. The best way to teach children is to lead by example. My youngest, who is nine, jumps to do anything I ask him to: take out the trash, clean up a spill, carry things in from the car, "I'll do it, Mommy!" My oldest, who is twelve, asked me if he could do anything to help after we had unloaded a vehicle full of a week's worth of vacation gear. My little one will leave notes outside my bedroom door for me to find when I get up. It's too sweet, making me feel loved and appreciated.

When everyone in the household adopts the mindset that you should help without being asked and show those you love how you feel by doing things to make their day better, the family bond becomes incredibly strong and filled with joy.

HE SAID

She: What is the key to a successful relationship?

He: Communication.

She: Well, yes, but I'm looking for something more specific and insightful, like what my advice is.

He: Give me a minute to think.

She: Well?

He: Getting into a relationship is like buying a new car. When you buy a new car, you assume it needs no maintenance, so you ignore the little things like oil changes or tire pressure because you assume that it's new and should just be perfect with no effort needed. But when these little issues get ignored for too long, they turn into big, expensive issues that could have easily been prevented with regular maintenance. Regular maintenance isn't that hard or expensive.

By the time the car needs serious repairs because of all the little maintenance that was ignored, you may not have the time, energy, or money to fix the car. When it gets to this point, it's just easier to get a new car than to put all the time, energy, and resources into the old one — the breakup.

If you had treated that car like an investment from the beginning, you could have kept it and been happy with it. It would have treated you well and done what you asked. When you invest time, money, and resources into something, you develop an emotional attachment to it. I do my own car repairs, and I take pride in doing that. It's hard for me to let go of my vehicles because I've put my own blood, sweat, time, and money into them, and I'm proud of the work and the vehicle.

She: Any other words of wisdom about how to be successful in a relationship?

He: Being with someone that allows you to be yourself and not to be nagged on or pushed and not belittled or made to feel less than gives a man the stability and security to follow a natural emotional maturity process that probably wouldn't be reached normally because he'd be suppressed and guarded.

I think emotional maturity is something a lot of women want in their men, but I don't think you can get that by pushing someone. A lot of women try to push for that, thinking that they can drive a man toward it, but it has to come naturally from the man. It has to be nurtured and allowed to happen at its own pace in order for it to be something that lasts a long time.

She: So, you're saying that you were not always emotionally mature in your past relationships?

He: No. Men aren't naturally emotionally mature; they are emotionally guarded, but women want that vulnerability out of them, and for them to do that, women need to back off. It will come when the man feels secure that she's not going to use it against him or that she's not going to fall back into those negative tendencies like nagging.

She: So, this is not normal behavior for you? To be the more emotionally mature one in the relationship?

He: It's not natural for most men at all.

She: Well, I know. That's why it's so shocking to me.

He: I don't think relationships ever get to the point where a man finds his emotional maturity. A lot of women say things like, "I want him to do this on his own," but a man won't do things on his own unless he is given the time and space to be able to think like that after he feels secure that he can become vulnerable and reach emotional maturity.

Relationships require regular, routine maintenance. I call my weekends to dye my hair and do my nails my "regularly scheduled maintenance." Anything that you expect to perform at its highest level will require maintenance.

Andy and I do relationship maintenance by performing little kind acts for each other every day, with or without being asked. We do it because we love each other so much, and love means putting the other person's happiness above your own. It IS about making a conscious effort each and every day to find a small way to make the other person's day better or easier. It's about sacrifice, but sacrifice for the right reasons. Sacrifices should not be made with the intention of claiming martyrdom and demanding the prize for being more unselfish in a relationship. Helping your partner achieve emotional maturity nirvana, however, requires counterintuitive measures. Easing up to get what you want seems like it won't work, but treating your partner with patience, love, and support will help him become who he needs to be for you both to be happy.

When you find the person who makes even the most selfish part of you want to make sacrifices every day just so the other person will smile or laugh or feel loved and cherished, you know you're in the right relationship with the right person. When you're exhausted, your partner needs something, and you muster enough energy to ask him how you can help simply because you hate to see him unhappy, you know it's right. When you make a conscious effort to change your negative reactions or behaviors because you know you need to show him how much you love and appreciate him, you know it's right. When you find yourself making the sacrifices and hard behavior corrections, you're in the perfect place to set yourself up for your own epic love story. You're with your person.

HE ASKED

1. Does the work you're putting into your relationship seem rewarding or more like a chore?

2. If it feels like a chore, could the reason be that your efforts are not being appreciated or reciprocated?

3. If you feel like you aren't being appreciated, are you being appreciative of the work your partner is putting into the relationship?

4. Would you be willing to go above and beyond your typical efforts to start the paying-it-forward positive momentum in your relationship?

Chapter 16: The Fairytale Future

Not every great love story will start with a made-for-TV Hallmark movie meet-cute, just like every epic meet-cute won't necessarily lead to a fairytale ending. And speaking of that cliché, there is no point in seeking the fairytale ending because finding your person isn't the end. It is the beginning of a beautiful journey through life together with your non-best-friend-love-of-your-life.

There are no guarantees that you'll find the love of your life, but I can guarantee that if you don't try your darndest every day of your relationship, you will never be successful at having the love of your life. Notice I said "having," not "meeting." You could very well meet the love of your life but not have the love of your life because you aren't ready: you may not be healed from past relationships, you may not be mature enough to be selfless, you may not have enough experience to recognize what's good and what isn't.

You must do your prep work beforehand to have that love story love. Make sure that you are emotionally stable, that you're healed from past relationships, and that you're aware of what your must-haves, must-not-haves, and nice-to-haves are. Make sure that you're able to be happy on your own before you even think about dating, regardless of your relationship status. Starting out a new relationship in a bad mental headspace will ensure that you won't be able to trust knowing whether or not you've found your person.

Yes, life is short, and people crave relationships and think they need to have them immediately and all the time. Even if your biological clock is ticking so loudly that you can barely hear, appeal to your logical side and look at approaching the process in the most efficient way. Do the work upfront and have your fairytale future instead of wasting six months at a time jumping from bad relationship to bad relationship. Each failure will not only leave you standing alone, but it will leave you holding one more piece of baggage until there's too much baggage to carry. If you do find yourself in failing relationships over and over and over again, you need to realize that the common factor in each failure is you. Stop blaming other people and take time to evaluate what you could have done better, even if doing better means you need to do better at partner selection.

I totally understand wanting to get back out there after a breakup, but you wouldn't go to a job interview without having researched the company or without having aligned your résumé skill set with the job requirements. Doing that kind of prep work for your career makes total sense to everyone, but anything personal or tied to emotions is subject to illogical decision-making.

When finding your person, always trust your gut, whether it's telling you you've found the one or throwing out little red flags.

Little red flags are like those cheap, spongy kids' toys that come in a little plastic pill that, when placed in a glass of water, expands to twenty times their original size. Intuition exists for a reason. Trust it.

If you find that one person you're attracted to, you trust intimately, you are selfless toward, and that you have good communication with, that's when you need to shift your mindset into how to keep that person and maintain a harmonious relationship. Start your relationship on the path to success by setting your expectations regarding division of labor, communication preferences, and intimacy expectations. Keep each other accountable for the expectations set from the beginning, and you won't end up feeling like you got baited and switched.

How many times do we have to hear that relationships take work to heed the advice? We all know it's true, yet so many relationships fail due to perceived laziness or avoidance of the hard conversations. So much sucking, but it's often from both sides.

Finding your person can often feel like home, and home is comfortable. Some degree of comfort is necessary in a relationship, but how comfortable were you when you were dating? Not very. If your goal is to be comfortable in your relationship, why do you miss those dating butterflies? Comfort leads to complacency, and complacency leads to taking things for granted. Taking things for granted leads to resentment, and resentment kills relationships. Take an adventure together, try a new restaurant, or learn something new together. Introducing something new or exciting into a comfortable relationship will bring back those butterflies that stem from the unknown.

Continue to explore new hobbies with or without your partner, keep in regular contact with friends and family, and don't forget to give your partner a break and a chance to miss you.

As you grow and change, keep communicating what you need from your partner to be happy and be open and receptive to what they need to be happy. Comfort in communication is the comfort you should seek, the respectful, safe place to talk about anything. Life will throw changes your way, but if you're on the same team, you can meet each challenge together.

Remind yourself that if you aren't perfect, you shouldn't expect your partner to be, especially with the stopsticks life throws in front of you at the last second. Give your partner grace when they're upset because, chances are, they're overreacting not because of you but because of the stress of life, kids, or work. In those moments when your first instinct is to match their intense temperament, take a deep breath and listen, ask what you can do to help, and love them at their worst.

The more you can retrain yourself to be the person you want to love you back, the healthier and happier your relationship will be.

Remind yourself that their little imperfections aren't personal. Their imperfections are simply part of who they are, and you love who they are. Forgive, forget, and build those bridges over the scorekeeping quicksand. Any negativity you can alleviate from your relationship, whether from yourself, your partner, or those pesky naysayers, will only leave more open space for you to grow in love together.

Love grows slowly over time and transforms from the butterflies and excitement of infatuation to security in being able to be yourself and knowing you'll be loved for it. Love is daily acts of kindness and selflessness. Love moves you to want to be the best version of yourself while inspiring your partner to do the same. In that evolution, you build a foundation of mutual respect. Love is in the details, in the moments we least expect it, in the brief kisses goodbye, in the treats for no reason, and in the words, "Can I help you?" The frozen grapes, the music, the sand vacuuming, the cola-flavored bottle caps, these little things put small scoops of sand in your bucket of love. They are the regular maintenance you are performing on your relationship vehicle to keep it healthy and running smoothly. To most people, those little things don't seem like much. However, when those little things are added up, they become the key to success in love and relationships.

No one ever looks back at their life and wishes they would have yelled more at their partner for leaving a light on or not making the bed correctly. No, you reflect and wonder why you didn't appreciate your partner more, why you didn't forgive their little mistakes, or why you didn't love them more freely, passionately, and unconditionally. Regrets are something you want to have the least of when you draw your last breath. Look ahead and try to think about what you may regret and make a course correction to make those changes now before it's too late.

No matter how long or short the time that you have with your love is, you know that there will be a day when one of you will pass on, so cherish each moment and every day with them. In your time together, spend more time loving than arguing, be selfless instead of selfish, and bask in the blessing of living a great love story. You will be one of the few lucky ones who climbed the relationship mountain and earned the coveted love-of-your-life badge. Wear it proudly and cherish it.

On your journey up that steep mountain, get out your old-school paper map and plot your path toward relationship success and a life lived without regrets. You are the only one who is accountable for your own actions, you are the only one who can change your future, and you are the only one in charge of your happiness, the compassion you show, the kindness you give, and the legacy of love you leave behind.

Epilogue

There have been several points in my relationship with Andy when I felt like we leveled up in a deeper connection and understanding of each other. Well, I think maybe it's more my feelings of leveling up than his. These milestones in our relationship have inspired and compelled me to dispense advice to my friends and now to you. I mean, if you found something great that you couldn't live without, wouldn't you want to tell the world and the people you care about so that they could have the chance to experience it, too?

Some of these moments of relationship enlightenment happened while writing this book, and some happened after the publishing process began. I think it's important to understand that no matter how well your relationship is working, there are always chances to suck less, learn more about your partner, and grow together.

Level Up 1: Road Trip Mind Probing

Once a year, Andy and I make the long trek south to visit his family in Iowa for Thanksgiving, and that trip means over seven hours trapped together during the peak time of day when his ADHD medication is working its darndest to help him focus. It's the perfect storm to probe his mind for the answers I can't get enough of.

During several of these first trips together, we would listen to a dating advice podcast, I would strategically use the topics they covered to address questions that I had about him and his past relationships. Outside of that vehicle entrapment, getting that information out of him was met with a great deal of resistance or running into his wall of blind secrecy.

Andy scoffed at the podcast on our trip south in November 2019, "We could do so much better than these two." Me being me, I pulled out a notebook and started writing down ideas. Nothing came of that idea session until the COVID-19 pandemic hit, and my Type A brain got bored and needed a new project. I recalled having heard somewhere that couples should have a shared hobby, and since Andy and I had pretty much nothing in common, I thought that there was no better time to start a podcast of our own than during a pandemic.

"Andy, I have decided that we should do a podcast," I said to him one day.

"I don't want to do that," he responded.

"Um, I distinctly remember discussing starting our own podcast on that trip to Iowa."

"I don't remember that," he stated.

"I have notes. Let me figure out what needs to be done to make it work, and then we can start," I giggled, knowing full well that we were about to start a new adventure together.

Level Up 2: Our Podcast

After doing a bit of research, I had our podcast platform ready to record. The *G.I. Joe and Barbie in Love* podcast was my way of interviewing my partner and getting to know his thoughts while also having a project to work on when there was not much else to do. Through the year of doing the podcast together, I learned a great deal about him, and I even saw a different side of him that I wouldn't have seen had we not done this project together. A few of the last episodes stemmed from ideas he had. He actually wrote the interviews, and I changed roles to become the interviewee. In our role reversal, I found a new respect for him as I watched him prepare for the podcast tapings.

That time shared together learning a new skill, working out the kinks, and reaping the reward of an end result that we could both be proud of was not only a way to make something good come out of something bad that was happening, but it almost became an additional support at the base of our relationship. I cherish that time in our life, and I'm thankful for what that endeavor taught me about him and how well we can work together toward the same goal.

Level Up 3: This Book

By this time, five years into being together, Andy knows that I always have to have one or two or three side projects going to keep my brain busy and learning. I hit a point in mid-2023 when I felt again that I needed a project. One morning, when I was on the treadmill, I decided I wanted to write a book.

Bursting into the bedroom where Andy was peacefully and unknowingly sleeping, I exclaimed, "Husband! I have come to a decision! I'm going to write a book."

"Okaaaaay," he replied groggily.

"Why are you responding like that? Don't you think that I'll do it?" I asked, annoyed that he wasn't more excited.

"I'm sleeping. I know you'll do it," he pacified and rolled over.

A week into writing this book, something happened, and I lost the outline of the chapters I wanted to cover. I freaked out, but in my scrambling to rewrite the notes I'd lost, I came up with a different idea for the direction of the book: maybe I should interview Andy for his perspective on each topic, kind of like a mini-podcast. He again resisted when I told him that I needed his input for my book.

"It's your book; why do I have to be part of it?" he asked, knowing that he likely didn't have a choice in the matter. "I don't see how interviews are going to work out in the book's flow."

"Never you mind; it will work. Trust me," I chimed.

We spent a lot of time at the beach in the short summers of Duluth, and I thought it would be a great place to do our book interviews while he was in a great mood. Through the discussions we had around the book's topics and through working through some of his issues with my use of his image and texts in my social media marketing plan, I had the strangest revelation . . .

My husband was way more emotionally mature than I was. He has lived most of his life trying to stay in the shadows. He has no social media for a reason, and my putting him out there freaked him out.

Apparently, he didn't think I was fully grasping how uncomfortable my use of his information on social media was, so he would say, "I knew that when I married you, you were always going to do what you want to," he explained.

"Well, I don't want this book about our successful relationship to lead to the downfall of our relationship," I answered as I started to worry.

"It's okay because I'll just be mad about it when I'm by myself. I'm also going to do what I want to do because that's what you do," he countered with a lightly veiled threat.

Because he didn't think I was fully grasping how what I was doing was making him feel, he decided to teach me a lesson that I had no idea was happening.

Below are our texts back and forth showing how much more mature he is than I am:

She: You still haven't really explained to me what you're talking about when you say stuff like, "I'll just do what I wanna do then." It's unnerving. I also don't like it when I feel like you think less of me for what I do or what I say.

He: I know. That is my way of sharing with you what it feels like to me having an online presence. It's the scary unknown. I don't know how to express it in words in a way to make you understand, so I showed you.

She: Seriously?!

He: Yes.

She: What would you propose I do to be able to successfully market my book about relationships that includes you then?

He: I don't want you to do anything. I want to support you. I just want you to understand that it isn't easy to deal with on my part. Sometimes, I feel like you think it's no big deal because it comes off mainstream, but for someone who spent his entire life trying to remain in the shadows, it's a lot to take in.

She: Okay, well, I can't fully enjoy what I'm doing if I know that it's making you feel like that.

He: Well, as long as you can show that you understand my apprehension about it and will respect the fact that it's not going to be what I want, I will endure it. I can ride out anything for you as long as it isn't assumed that I have to enjoy it the way you do. In other words, you can't expect me to get as excited about it as you are. You have to accept that my support comes from my acceptance to endure because I love you. Any time you don't feel supported, I want you to know without a doubt that I am absolutely supporting you.

She: Thank you for expressing that. I love you so much. I appreciate your support and sacrifice.

He: It's what I signed up to do.

Touché, husband, touché! For the man who lives in the moment and who can't plan an hour in the future, he had been setting me up to learn this lesson for weeks! It's so painful for me to realize that he knows me better than I know myself . . . probably because he's a quiet observer and a good listener, but still. Maybe I should have known all along that he would always be a step ahead of me in emotional maturity because he had more experience in more relationships, or maybe because he told me he read *Men Are from Mars, Women Are from Venus* after his divorce when this therapist told him to read it. He doesn't read. He hates it.

When I was writing this book, he forewarned, "Don't make it too long because I'm going to have to read it." Oh, Andy.

Level Up 4: Full Circle, But Still Learning

On our most recent road trip to Iowa, we were working on the end-of-chapter questions for Andy to ask. With plans to meet for lunch an hour away, I had carved out two hours for us to work on the second half of the book's questions. I was stressed about getting the edits done, and Andy was getting frustrated with his brain for not giving me the questions for the ends of the chapters.

After two unproductive hours, we got in the car to meet some family for lunch, but I was so angry, and he was frustrated. The ironic part about the situation was that the chapter we were stuck on was the chapter about communication, and we were communicating horribly. I was taking out my frustration on him because of my manuscript timeline and because his brain wasn't working like mine.

"At least I'm still trying," he reasoned with me. "I just can't make what's in my head make sense. I'm not mad at you; I'm mad at myself for not being able to give you what you need," he confessed.

Did I say, "I know, and I love you for that"? No, I was sucking at taking my own advice about communication because I couldn't step away from my emotions in order to reply with rationality and logic.

On our drive back to the hotel after lunch with his family, Andy said, "When we get back to the hotel, I'm going to sit down and write the questions. I want to help you, but my mind wasn't working earlier," he noted.

"Don't you have those quick-acting ADHD meds that you can take to help you focus?" I asked.

"Oh yeah, I forgot about those," he admitted.

When Andy was re-medicated and we were back at the hotel, we found our way back to collaborating calmly, and the rest of the questions were completed within an hour.

"I'm sorry I was so mad at you this morning," I apologized with my tail between my legs. "I was being a bad wife."

"I'm not upset about it. I know that you get like that when you put too much on your plate, and I was prepared for it," he explained.

"I love you," I told him as I rocked up on my tiptoes to kiss him. "You're such a good husband."

The final leveling-up also happened during this trip. While working on the edits, Andy opened up about something that I'm not sure he would have shared had it not been triggered by the conversations about the book's content:

He: I don't think that I understood how good our relationship was until our wedding. It didn't hit me emotionally until then.

She: The wedding that you didn't want to have?

He: I don't think that I had conceptualized it until it opened up to me at the wedding, and I was like, "Holy crap, this is pretty good!"

She: At the wedding!?

He: Yeah.

She: (*Shocked*) WHAT are you talking about?! I don't understand what's happening.

He: I loved you, and I was okay with getting married, but I don't think that until we did get married and the ceremony happened that I realized it was pretty good. I can't explain it more; it just hit me at that point when the dots just connected, and I knew it was better than I thought it could be.

She: Was that AFTER your vows?

He: No, it was seeing you, and the whole deal with Nolan (I put a photo of his best friend who had passed on the front chair at the wedding) ripped it all open, and I lost control.

She: Oh, so it ripped a hole in your wall then, huh? Is that what happened?

He: Probably. But I'm just saying that up until that point, I thought I had a handle on a lot of what was going on, but I don't think that I actually understood until then. It's not something I talk about a lot.

She: I know because I haven't heard this before. It's been a year since our wedding.

He: Well, there's no reason to really talk about it.

She: Why WOULDN'T there be a reason to talk about it? It seems really paramount to me.

He: I just assumed that you feel the same way about it that I do.

She: Why would you assume that?

He: Because (*pause*), I just don't see how you couldn't. It's a personal journey of someone's awakening.

She: For you! Yeah, because you know what's funny to me? I noticed a shift in your emotions after the wedding; I told people this. You seemed to take a more loving parenting role with my kids, and you seemed different with me. I kept telling people, "He's different but in a good way," and I didn't see that coming. Is that what happened?

He: Yeah, when you can see in front of you that love is better than you thought it could be, especially if you work so hard in your life to be happy and to have peace, and you finally see what that looks like, and the wedding was the solidifying of that, it's pretty powerful because I don't think most people ever get to that.

Most people are so worried about meaningless stuff that they don't ever realize that it can be better than they think it can be. People have said that to me, and I've been like, "Yeah, whatever! That sounds stupid." But when it hits you, it's like, "You'll see."

It's not the same, but I would compare it to a lot of people who find Christ for the first time. That realization of "holy crap, this guy did this for me?" is super powerful. It almost chokes you off because it's so powerful. That's the only thing I can compare it to.

The relationship we have is the first thing that I can look back at in my life that's better than I could have imagined.

When I bought a motorcycle, I thought, "This is going to be so awesome!" but then it faded. You self-medicate, you buy things, you do all these things that you think are the perfect thing, and it never amounts to what you think it's going to be. You always feel somewhat unsatisfied.

For us, things were the same before the wedding in the things that you did that made my life easier, and it's easy to fall into that trap of taking things for granted, but now, I constantly think about that kind of stuff like, "Wow, this is nice," or "This is really cool that this happens like this."

She: How are you able to do that? Most people go the opposite way when something is happening for so long, like, "That's just how it is now, and . . ."

He: Because I'm in the moment. As someone who always lives in the moment, I feel like my life is always pretty good. Even if something happens to me, like my boiler going down, it seems like nothing because I'm still pretty happy.

I find myself being less and less stressed the longer that we're together because I'm always happy. Internally, I'm constantly reminded of how peaceful and how good I have it. From any aspect of your life, you cannot understand how good that is until you're in that position. There are very few things that I feel emotionally tied to, but that emotional intelligence of understanding where that peace comes from and having appreciation for that is a natural process that comes from the things you do to put me in a place like that.

She: You don't think it's a lot of work being married to me?

He: Not really.

She: I think most people would fear that.

When I read the first draft of this book to my husband on one of our long car rides south to Iowa, I asked him, "What was your favorite chapter?" I expected him to pick one that was funny.

He responded, "The one about what love is."

"Really?!" I replied with confusion. "Why?"

"Because it got me thinking back through our relationship, and it made me a little emotional."

Again, there's another instance of my sucking because I underestimated my husband yet again in the depth of emotion and communication that he has in our relationship. I realize almost once a month or every other week that I am so lucky to have found a man who understands me and loves me so much that he's willing to make constant sacrifices to support me, my dreams, and my happiness. And while he may make some objections to the things I want, like putting his foot down about not wanting to wear the pink tie I bought for the cover shoot for this book, we always find a way to work through any hurdles with respect and love because we both understand what we share and how rare it is to find.

Andy always tells me that women will need to get over the fact that they will be the ones who have to put more work into a relationship to make it successful, but I'm not sure that's true. A woman can put a ton of effort in, but unless her partner is meeting her halfway at each step, they won't be able to move forward together and at the same pace.

Relationships are complicated, and there is no one correct path to finding that true connection: the love that brings peace, the love that makes the hard times seem like nothing, the love that feels solid and constant and that infuses your life with support and happiness. Be happy, my new friends. Never lose hope, and never stop trying. The success in love we have found is something we hope that our experiences and advice will help you achieve. While it may take time and effort to get there, it will be so much better and so much easier than you could ever have imagined.

Bibliography

Helplama. 2023. "Beauty Industry Revenue and Usage Statistics 2023." Helplama.com. July 3, 2023. https://helplama.com/beauty-industry-revenue-usage-statistics/.

"Skincare Market." n.d. Allied Market Research. Accessed December 22, 2023. https://www.alliedmarketresearch.com/skincare-market-A31878.

Cyndi Lewis was born in South Korea, was adopted to Wisconsin, and currently lives in Duluth, MN. Her decades of writing marketing copy, blogs, press releases, magazine articles, and short stories have sharpened her writing skills. Cyndi's passion is advising on subject matters that she is successful in. *Suck Less at Love: She Said, He Said Advice on Relationships* is her first self-help book, but she is working on more for the series. Learn more about her at:
www.cyndlewisauthor.com
Instagram & Facebook @cyndilewisauthor